Business Lessons from Japan

What I Learned as an Entrepreneur from Samurai, Sushi Chefs, and Earthquakes

by Atom Alex Helling

BUSINESS LESSONS FROM JAPAN:
What I Learned As An Entrepreneur from Samurai, Sushi Chefs, and Earthquakes

Copyright © 2014 Atom Alex Helling

All rights reserved.

No part of this publication may be reproduced or transmitted in any form or by any means, mechanical or electronic, including photocopying or recording, or by any information storage and retrieval system, or transmitted by email without permission in writing from the publisher.

While all attempts have been made to verify the information provided in this publication, neither the author nor the publisher assumes any responsibility for errors, omissions, or contrary interpretations of the subject matter herein.

This book is for entertainment purposes only. The views expressed are those of the author alone and should not be taken as expert instruction or commands. The reader is responsible for his or her own actions. The information in this book does not constitute legal, tax or accounting advice. It provides general information, based on the author's personal experience, which is not a substitute for obtaining the advice of a competent professional, for example a licensed attorney, law firm, accountant or financial adviser. In no event will the author or the publisher be liable for any loss or damage whatsoever arising from the use of the information in this book.

Adherence to all applicable laws and regulations, including international, federal, state and local governing professional licensing, business practices, advertising, and all other aspects of doing business in the US, Canada, or any other jurisdiction is the sole responsibility of the purchaser or reader.

Neither the author nor the publisher assumes any responsibility or liability whatsoever on the behalf of the purchaser or reader of these materials.

Any perceived slight of any individual or organization is purely unintentional.

ISBN-10: 1502588560

ISBN-13: 978-1502588562

DEDICATION

To all my friends who helped me on my journey in this exciting and beautiful country.

末代まで感謝致します。

CONTENTS

	Introduction	5
1	How to Establish Yourself	17
2	Networking and Communication	37
3	Business Meetings	47
4	The Business Lunch or Dinner	53
5	Deal-making	67
6	How To Manage People and Projects	79
7	Productivity Hacks	87
8	How To Spot and Avoid Trouble	99
9	Damage Control	107
10	My Main Takeaways	111
	Epilogue : Beyond Japan	113
	Appendix: A Primer on Japan	120
	About the Author	121
	Thank You	122
	Stay in Touch	123
	Other Books by Atom Alex Helling	124

INTRODUCTION: FROM CALIFORNIA TO THE LAND OF THE RISING SUN

Japanese people are rigid, strict, polite, passive, disciplined and respectful. This is what my neighbor told me the other day. She has never been in Japan. Obviously, there is no need to travel there to have a strong opinion about the Japanese. Their food is a staple all around the world today, and all of us have tasted sushi or some variety of a ramen or soba dish. Japanese movies, animation, manga comics and games have made a splash far beyond the borders of that little rock at the far Eastern edge of the globe. The media likes to report about its humanoid dancing robots and other technological inventions. And once in a while there is a consumer trend that takes over the world and then flames out fast. Or does anyone still have a *Tamagotchi* [1]? With all this buzz, Japan has managed to be on everybody's radar.

At the same time, the country is a paradox, mysterious and misunderstood. Its language is complicated, and so are its mannerisms, customs and even its history. The image the media portrays is quite different from the real thing. This becomes apparent when one visits for a longer time and begins to interact with the Japanese on a level deeper than a tourist. Doing business there is a Pandora's box that some find fascinating, others utterly frustrating. I have scratched my head many times in the three years I was living in Tokyo. So what is it that makes the land of the rising sun so unique?

What This Book Is and What It Is Not

Before we examine the answer to this question, let me first outline what this book is about. Even though we will get a first-hand look at the customs and business culture of the Japanese, this book is more than a reference for business etiquette or how-to guide. Next to describing how they approach certain situations, it will explain the lessons I learned from living and working there, and how they can be valuable in any other place in the world, in any line of work. If you are relatively new to Japan, I recommend you have a look in the Appendix of this book, where I give a Primer on Japan. This puts some of the strange customs and curiosities into perspective. After reading this book , you will understand how I experienced the Japanese in business relationships, and the takeaways I drew from my adventures that still stick with me today. Think about these business lessons as a way to find solutions to challenges from a Japanese

---

[1] Wikipedia. Tamagotchi. https://en.wikipedia.org/wiki/Tamagotchi.

perspective. They are global in scope, regardless of their origin. I am no longer living in Tokyo, but I still use many of the strategies that I learned there.

These observations are my personal viewpoints, and I am sure some people would disagree with my interpretations. I backed them up with other sources when it made sense, but they all have their origins in situations I experienced first hand in Japan. I hope they show you a new angle to tackle situations in your own business with a fresh approach. The Japanese approach will be exotic and unexpected, and that is perhaps exactly what a particular challenge needs.

How I Came to Live in Japan

In my early twenties, I started an advertising agency and music production company in Switzerland. After a lucky exit, I moved to Los Angeles, where I was an active entrepreneur and a music composer of film scores and pop songs. Eventually, I landed a production deal with one of the largest record labels in the world. If you have an interest in my adventures in Los Angeles and the business lessons I learned there, you find them in my book *Business Lessons from Hollywood*.[2]

In my studio in Venice, California, I had started a project together with a Japanese songwriter that unexpectedly took off in Japan. When that happened, the time seemed right for something new, and I moved to Tokyo to focus on that particular project. Even though it came to a halt in unforeseen ways six months into my stay, I ended up living in Japan for almost three years. In that time, my life took an entirely different direction, mainly because I had to leave my comfort zone and stretch myself beyond what I thought possible. My adventures in Japan helped me reinvent my business. I enrolled in the international program at the London School of Economics (LSE) to finish my degree in economics, and then went on to consult private and corporate clients in entrepreneurial finance. Even though it was hard for most of the time, it was worth it and I would do it again if I had a choice.

It is safe to say that my career followed an unconventional path. Usually, it goes something like this: After a young banker has made millions in a hedge fund, he retires to the beach in California and starts writing songs. I know several people with such a story. But I did the opposite: After success as a songwriter and creative entrepreneur, I left the entertainment industry, went back to school in my thirties, and started a career in finance and

---

[2] Helling, Atom Alex. Business Lessons from Hollywood: What I Learned as an Entrepreneur in the Capital of Entertainment (2014).
http://www.atomalex.com/business-lessons-hollywood.

economics. Without moving to Japan, I would never have done this. The result of this journey is a unique perspective on business and entrepreneurship. Being native to both the performing arts and quantitative finance has helped me enormously, especially when it comes to analyzing situations from different viewpoints. This integrated perspective is the primary strength of the business lessons in this book. They unite diverse angles and wrap them up in a single conclusion that makes sense without much domain knowledge.

What Would Japan Do?

Before I moved to Tokyo for good, I was under the impression that I already knew how things worked. I had visited Japan about a dozen times before. Having stayed at people's homes several times, I was vaguely familiar with Japanese domestic life. And I had built a small network over the years with local entrepreneurs and business people that I had kept in touch with. My experiences made me believe I was well equipped for business and life in Japan. However, in the first weeks of living there it dawned on me that I had barely scratched the surface. As a foreigner who did not speak the language and barely understood the culture, I stumbled into amusing and less amusing situations that were the motivation to write this book. With these business lessons from Japan, I hope to share some of my observations with you. I hope you will find them helpful in your own line of work, wherever you are.

Atom Alex Helling,
Hong Kong, October 2014

ATOM ALEX HELLING

CHAPTER 1: HOW TO ESTABLISH YOURSELF

When you start a new business or begin to work in a new city, you need to establish yourself first. You need to tell others about your talents and your plans. Every new situation comes with challenges. As often, this is less about exactly *what* you do, but *how* you do it. In this chapter, we examine some of the approaches that have helped me set up shop in Japan. You will also learn a little more about my own adventure and what exactly I did in Japan. The lessons in this chapter are helpful to navigate situations anywhere in the world, whenever you need to master difficult territory, customs, or personalities, or when you need a different perspective on a particular challenge.

Check Your Assumptions

I was living in a bubble when I moved to Japan. The contract I had signed with a large record label put my head firmly in the clouds. Whenever I visited Tokyo, a limousine with a chauffeur in white gloves would await me at Narita airport. In a Mercedes Benz S-Class 600, he would take me straight to a suite in the Park Hyatt in Shinjuku, the hotel in which the movie *Lost in Translation*[3] was filmed. I lived like this for a few months on the record company's dime. Then the project came to an abrupt end, and I learned what life in Japan was really like.

Foreigners called to work in Japan often benefit from similar arrangements. A friend of mine managed a hedge fund for a large American investment bank. While he was stationed in Tokyo, he made a million dollars a year in salary, plus a living cost adjustment of a hundred thousand dollars per year. Being a single guy, he saved all of his salary and lived on the adjustment alone, walking away a multi millionaire after a few short years. Another friend held a position as a diplomat at an embassy. His six-digit salary went straight to his tax-exempt bank account. He had zero expenses for food and lived in the ambassador's quarters in the fanciest district in Tokyo without spending a dime.

Both quit their jobs and ventured out on their own to make the really big bucks, or better: they tried to. The hedge fund manager started his own fund. It folded after six months. This left him almost bankrupt, with an expired work visa, and no prospect of finding new employment in Japan. After trying to spend his way out of the downward spiral, he reluctantly

---

[3] Coppola, Sofia. Lost in Translation (2003).
http://www.imdb.com/title/tt0335266.

went back to New York and took on a desk job as a banker. The diplomat suffered a similar fate. His consulting agency failed to gain any traction, and he returned into government service in a different country just a year later. They had enjoyed privileges as well-protected expats, but that had nothing to do with starting a business on their own in Japan. When they tried, they were unable to make a dent.

But not only high-rollers underestimate Japan. Entrepreneurs, university graduates and artists are prone to do the same. Based on good memories from prior visits, they arrive in the country with unrealistic expectations. After they have found an apartment (not easy for a foreigner at a reasonable price), they start job hunting. Some of them speak perfect Japanese, have a Masters' degree in Japan studies or another highly specialized field. Still, they struggle to find work. After several months with a high burn rate, they finally settle in a job at a language school. Or they may work as a barista. Landing work in a Japanese company as a foreigner is extremely difficult, even for those who are highly qualified. Most expats find themselves humbled a few short months later. Instead of burdening yourself with high expectations, better go with the flow and see what Japan has in store for you. It might be different from what you imagined.

I tried to force my expectations into existence as well. Having started successful companies in Europe and America, I assumed I would be equally triumphant in Japan. Naturally, I thought I would pick up where I left after my music project tanked, but that was not meant to be. Six months passed and no one seemed interested in my ideas and what I had to offer. I slowly ran out of money. When I abandoned my expectations and started enjoying the experience, a new world opened up for me. I started doing things that cost nothing or very little, met a lot of interesting new people, and travelled through the country by bus and bicycle. I stocked vending machines with soda bottles, stayed at a monastery in the mountains and packaged green tea in a factory. Eventually, I went back to school which kick-started an entirely new career for me. This only happened because my initial plans failed to materialize.

I talked about this winding road of a resume with my Japanese friends, just to find out that they found it perfectly normal. Superstition and mysticism are wide-spread in Japan. Sure, people plan their life just as anywhere else. But when unexpected setbacks happen, they are quick to accept them. Destiny is beyond one's control in Japan, so people keep an open mind about what the heavens have in store. This is somewhat at odds with the Western idea where everybody is responsible for his own fate. When things refuse to work out as we want, we often tighten up and try to force destiny back on the trajectory we had in mind. By all means, plan for your future. But when things become stuck, a hands-off approach can introduce a radical perspective with unexpected results.

Business Lesson

When things go great at the present, it is easy to assume everything will work out perfectly from here on. Your assumptions may be wrong. Accept that life may have something else in store for you, and be open for unexpected opportunities.

Be a Rock Star

Unless you have a strong track record as an entrepreneur abroad, starting a company from scratch in Japan will be a challenge. First-time founders can achieve success almost anywhere with a good idea, enough determination and sweat equity. I proved this several times with my own ventures, first in Europe and then in America. However, Japan is a different beast. Your hard work contributes only a small part to your success. What matters more is the support network and the Japanese connections that can open doors for you. The locals start building these connections in college, which is the reason they study so hard in high school. Unless they attend a prestigious academic institutions, their life will hardly ever advance past a certain pay grade.

The best reference in Japan is the University of Tokyo, or *Todai*. Most government employees, a coveted job in Japan, graduate there. The private Keio University is the second-best choice. Several prime ministers and successful entrepreneurs are Keio alumni. When the Japanese study at one of these colleges, they meet the Japanese upper class who can make things happen for them. As a foreigner, you will rarely have access to these networks, and competing with Japanese entrepreneurs from the ground level up will leave you at a disadvantage.

Things look different if you come from a position of strength. You will then start out several levels above the average Japanese entrepreneur, and doors open for you rapidly. This is the case if you have a proven track record of success outside of Japan, something most native entrepreneurs struggle to achieve. The preferential treatment of successful foreigners is most evident with celebrities. If you appear on the cover of international magazines, wrote a global smash hit or directed a blockbuster movie, the Japanese will welcome you with open arms. If you had a business success, for example, if you sold your company in an eight- or nine-figure deal, you will also be ahead of the pack in Japan. However, what really matters is that you make your success visible. Rock star business people and entrepreneurs give interviews, write books, appear on TV and in magazines. Fashion yourself as a celebrity in demand. Otherwise, you will have a hard time climbing the ranks.

I noticed this first hand with my own music project. Together with a Japanese co-founder (a graduate from Keio university), I started it in my little studio in Venice and saw it mushroom to global proportions in only six months. We landed over a hundred press articles and interviews, numerous photo shoots, concerts around the globe, endorsements and licensing deals. A Japanese record label paid top dollar to sign a four-album production deal with us. When we visited Tokyo, doors flung open and we found ourselves in meetings with Japanese movie and pop stars. We were highly visible and had achieved something that many Japanese entertainers only dream about: Success in America. This was my ticket to doing business in Japan. Years before, I had tried unsuccessfully to get the attention of record labels in Tokyo. They told me to first achieve success elsewhere and then come back to Japan. They were right, this is exactly how things work there. As a rock star, the sky is the limit. When you are in the same boat as everybody else, nothing will happen.

Business Lesson

Always enter new markets from a position of strength. Spend time to build your reputation before you approach important business partners. It is not just your product or your ideas that make them want you, but also your status as a celebrity and rock star.

Avoid Blending in Too Much

A friend of mine teaches German as a professor at Kyoto university. He has been living there for close to twenty years, his wife is Japanese, and his children attend the local schools. As a hobby, he performs classical Japanese music on the *shakuhachi* flute. He is also a connoisseur of *No* theater, a form of masked Japanese performance play dating back to the fourteenth century. If anyone can pass as Japanese, then it is him. When I visited him in Kyoto, he gave me a little city tour. Before we started, we went to the local tourist office to get some maps. I was stunned when he addressed the staff in heavily-accented English, posing as a tourist. He could have spoken accent-free Japanese with them, on the same level of proficiency like a native. When I asked him why he chose to speak English with the staff, I learned something interesting.

"I always pretend to be a tourist. Many foreigners try to be more Japanese than the locals. But at the end of the day, the Japanese will never accept them as one of their own. In all the years I have been living here, I still feel I don't belong. If you try to blend in too much, it's only to your disadvantage."

This was news to me. I had tried to do everything perfectly, practiced greeting in front of the mirror and learned some of the most common phrases in Japanese to accommodate my business partners. Every foreigner who has lived in Japan for a while has adopted Japanese mannerisms. Among them is tilting your head in a certain way to signal your disapproval, slightly bowing if you cross people in the supermarket, and apologizing when you enter a shop. This happens naturally until you become aware that nobody expects you to conform to all the rules. Of course, you should avoid coming across as rude or inconsiderate, but you also have some leeway. When you blend in too much, you will lose what makes you unique.

Think about it this way: Why does a Japanese company hire foreigners in the first place? So that they adapt perfectly and become indistinguishable from their own staff? A Japanese company is less interested in your dancing to their tune. Instead they expect you to teach them what you know. This demands that you keep your integrity and your edge.

Without knowing it, I had lost some of that edge in the first weeks of living in Japan. Like most newcomers, I was proudly soaking up the new rules like a sponge. Over time, this became confusing and I felt my confidence slipping. The Japanese habits I had adopted voluntarily and involuntarily seemed fake, and I decided to reclaim my ways of doing business that made me unique. Among them was a certain authority when I spoke with people. Being too polite was the wrong strategy, and it made communications more complicated. When I stopped it, I ended up getting much more done. The opportunity to be *not* Japanese is exclusively reserved for foreigners. Instead of giving it up they should celebrate it and use it to their advantage.

Business Lesson

By trying to blend in you lose your edge. Observe some of the local customs but also make use of the wild card you have as an outsider. Make it a point to not obey all the rules. As long as you stay friendly and polite, you get away with much more than you think.

Speak Your Language

Learning Japanese is fun. We all can say a few basic phrases, like *domo arigato, mushi mushi,* or *konnichi-wa*. When you visit a foreign country, most guides suggest you learn the most common greetings, thank you, where is the restroom, and so on. This makes sense for a tourist who needs to get around where nobody understands his native tongue. However, in a business setting, I find having a rudimentary grasp of a foreign language is not all that helpful. It can even be counterproductive. Let's examine why.

Imagine you are working as a contractor with a Japanese company. The company has invited you to visit their headquarters in Tokyo, and you happily oblige. On the plane, you pick up a few sentences to demonstrate your good will to blend in. When you meet with the company staff, you test your new knowledge. You greet them with the few Japanese words you know, garner some laughs, and apologize for not speaking the language better. This is what ninety-nine percent of people do. Without knowing it, they are undermining themselves.

Ask yourself again why the foreign company has hired you: To do things their way or your way? Obviously, they need foreign expertise, which is why they flew you in. They want *you* to lead *them*, not the other way around. Learning a few phrases and greeting them with bad pronunciation works to your disadvantage here. It makes you look like an amateur (which you are, in the foreign language). Better let your actions speak. Lead them to success with determination. Impose your business methods with confidence, demonstrate your expertise, and speak in your native language to them.

Not only does rudimentary knowledge of a language lower your profile, it can also land you in hot water. After I had signed my record deal in Japan, I and the team from the label met with support staff, agencies and managers in Tokyo for several weeks. On one occasion, we had a dinner with the owner of a talent management company in Tokyo. Their client roster included most famous actors, singers, comedians and other personalities in Japan. The principal was a middle-aged man in a tailored suit. During dinner, he told a story about buying out another agency. Everybody was revering the business genius of the man. His story about paying a very high amount of money for the other agency was indeed awe-inspiring. I felt I should express my admiration with a Japanese word I had recently picked up: *Ganbatte*. My Japanese friends had taught me this word to congratulate others when they did something right. As I blurted out my *ganbatte*, the person sitting next to the agency boss spewed the water he was just drinking across the entire table. Everybody stiffened up, and the man's mood darkened. My Japanese business partner immediately launched into an explanation of what I really meant, with pearls of sweat forming on her forehead. What had I done wrong? I was simply meaning to express that the agency had done a smart business deal. My partner told me later that this word is something you tell a child when he manages to accomplish a minor task. Like taking a few steps without falling down or playing a piece of music without screwing up. In effect, I was belittling the efforts of that agency boss, not complimenting him.

Such twists are common in Japanese. Words have alternative meanings that will never occur to you. Had I known it, I would have kept my mouth shut. When you try to gain respect in business in a foreign country, better speak English. It takes years to master the intricacies of the most foreign languages, especially in formal conversation. The pronunciation is often not that difficult, but when it comes to the hidden meaning and formalities with addressing those above or below you in status, there are countless pitfalls. Better steer clear of this minefield.

Business Lesson

On international business, present yourself as an expert in your field. Flawed and rudimentary knowledge of a foreign language undermines your status. Using foreign phrases might seem cute, but better avoid it. You may be saying the exact opposite of what you intend to bring across.

Be Open for the Unexpected

Intending to study at a Japanese university, a friend of mine had moved to Tokyo. Let's call him C. Today he is a fashion model in demand for high-end shows and photo shoots with the largest Japanese brands. How did all of this happen? Here is his story. Enter C.

"I was always a fan of all things Japan since a young age. Manga, anime, martial arts and the language fascinated me. I studied Japanese in Germany at university but wanted to deepen my knowledge by living and studying in Tokyo for a year. A week after I had settled in with another student in a tiny apartment on the outskirts of Tokyo, a girl approached me in a café in Harajuku, Tokyo's fashion district. She said she was a scout for a modeling agency and gave me an invite for a casting the following day. All this sounded like a joke to me, but I showed up at the agency for the casting. My looks are average, and I have no idea what they saw in me. I had never stood on a stage, let alone modeled before in my life. Apparently, they found me ideally suited for a campaign. A few days later, a minibus picked me up at my apartment, and we drove to a photo studio for the shoot. An interpreter told me what to do in front of the camera, which was basically standing around looking bored wearing jeans and white T-shirts. At the end of the day they drove me home and gave me an envelope. It contained 100,000 yen in cash (about US$1,000). A week later I landed another gig, and then another one. From there it continued, and I signed with a talent agency. I have been living in Japan for three years now just bought a condo in the middle of the city. I have barely had a day off. As long as this lasts, I will go with it. There is still plenty of time to go back to school later."

Quite a story, huh? Even though I did not get a modeling contract, my life took unexpected turns as well. When things did not turn out as expected, I could have packed my bags and returned home. That I stayed and went with the flow despite the fact that I had no idea where the journey went turned out to be a good decision.

Business Lesson

When unexpected opportunities come along, keep an open mind. Go with the flow for a while and see where it leads you. You can still turn around and do what you initially intended. But if you close yourself off to a chance, it may never return.

CHAPTER 2: NETWORKING AND COMMUNICATION

A strong network is key to business success. But how do you build one from scratch in a foreign country? Customs and communication patterns are distinctly different as soon as you leave America and Europe. To network effectively, it is important you familiarize yourself with the culture of the new place you try to establish yourself in. Instead of playing exactly by the rulebook, it is often better if you bend the rules a bit to your advantage. This is one of the few advantages you have as a fish out of the water. But before you can break the rules of networking and communication, you need to know them. This is what this chapter is about.

Activate All Contacts, Even Those On the Periphery

I usually combine trips to foreign countries with new projects or other business interests. The idea to visit a new place often comes from something I read about it, or a story that someone told me. When it seems interesting, I follow up by gathering first-hand intelligence on the ground. Research and network building excursions are what I do, not holidays or tourism. The last time I went abroad just to relax was when I was ten years old. Since then I have always tried to learn something new or meet people, no matter where I go.

I visited Japan for the first time after I met a Japanese exchange student in political science in Los Angeles. This was the first Japanese person I ever had a longer conversation with, and what he told me about the country and its cultural fabric sounded interesting. I felt I wanted to explore it further and booked a ten-day trip to Tokyo. This student was my only connection to the country. He was studying abroad when I visited, and he knew few people outside of his university in South Japan. None of my other friends had ever been there, so I needed to look elsewhere to get introductions.

A week before the flight I had exactly zero meetings lined up for my upcoming trip. It so happened that I attended a bachelor's party in Las Vegas with about twenty other guys from Los Angeles. By pure coincidence, there were two Japan experts in the group: One music industry lawyer with contacts at some record labels, and one guy who had actually lived there as a teenager. Both of them had interesting stories to tell and plenty of contacts in Tokyo. Even though I had just met them, they introduced me to about ten different people via email. I managed to meet them all when I was in town. Those were excellent contacts, and I felt like a master networker despite the fact that all of this was the result of two incidental encounters in Las Vegas.

When you tap your existing networks for introductions abroad, the best contacts may come from the periphery. Feel free to ask people to help even if you just met them. I am always surprised by the chance meetings that spring from the most unlikely situations.

Business Lessons

When you need introductions, ask anyone you meet to suggest them for you. As long as you come across as trustworthy and professional, they will often open their address book. Do the same when someone asks you. This builds goodwill that you may depend on later.

Look for Powerful Introducers

When your contacts have set you up with business introductions, it is time to follow through with meetings. I always met with everyone who came recommended by people in my network, and it has worked well for me. Of course, some of the meetings went nowhere, but there is always something to learn in any circumstance. Some of the chance encounters will be golden. According to the 80/20 rule, twenty percent of the connections you make will generate eighty percent of your business volume. It is these twenty percent that you should be interested in. When you build a network from scratch, finding them is a numbers game. The more people you meet, the more of these powerful contacts you will end up with in the end. It is as simple as that.

After taking a few meetings, you will have filtered out those people with whom you immediately had a good rapport. Concentrate on them, and ask them to activate their local networks for you as well. When doing business in Japan, you will find that the Japanese often care more about who introduced you than what exactly you are doing. Trying to build connections on merit and talent alone is futile. Your network and social standing are just as important because they validate your character as a potential business partner. Japanese always look for validation by others. When they check that box, the relationship can continue.

It is now time to introduce a Japanese philosophy that we will meet repeatedly in this book: The concept of *wa*, which translates into "harmony." It is the emphasis on loyalty and consensus within a group. Emotional support and a long-term perspective, both in business and personal relationships, are important in Japan. Other Asian countries have similar philosophies, such as *guanxi* in China, or *inhwa* in Korea. When you do business in Asia, you need to understand how these ideas influence business practice and communication patterns. The Japanese *wa* has its origins in traditional family values. When someone breaks the rules and disturbs the harmony, a higher-up brings him or her back into line. Businesses encourage *wa* with security, predictability and life-long employment. This fosters strong associations with colleagues who pull together as a team.

Why is this important to know? Japanese people avoid taking risks that have the potential to disrupt *wa*. Since foreigners have no track record or traditional family ties in Japan, the next best thing is the person who made the connection. When he or she has established *wa* with the Japanese counterparty, this will reflect positively on you. Being introduced by people with a high status in society can therefore go a long way in Japan. When someone connects you with others, pay attention to how they are perceived by those you meet. This can make or break a relationship right at the beginning.

Business Lessons

Carefully vet the people you meet and look for the most powerful influencers and connectors. Ask them to introduce you to their local networks. If they have a good reputation, this will help you advance faster in building your network.

Network Up, Not Down

Out of my first trip to Tokyo came many great connections with entrepreneurs and business people. This was a consequence of pure chance and guts to ask some people I had just met to introduce me to their friends. When I later visited Japan again, I was able to tap into my extended network and managed to have a good group of friends in the country when I finally moved there. I was lucky that I got on the right track right from the beginning. I only realized this later.

To meet with high-powered locals is definitely the preferred strategy when building your Japanese network. It is also the most demanding one, as there are countless little rules and customs to observe that can make or break the relationship right at the beginning. We will encounter most of them in the course of this book. Meeting foreigners and expats is much easier. There is an immediate rapport when you are both outsiders. Stories about mishaps and strange encounters are amusing, and every expat has plenty of them to tell. Even though it was fun to meet with them socially, I have never met a foreigner who could really help me in Japan. Most of them were living in a bubble (just like me when I moved there). As foreign experts in Western multinationals, they enjoy special status. On the other hand, none of them had achieved success with their own business. They were in no position to help me move my venture forward and often lacked the local connections or the insight into how things really worked on the ground. When you meet someone, ask yourself if you would exchange places with that person. Has that person reached a goal that you aspire to? If the answer is no, then why should you ask them for advice?

When venturing out in a new field or location, team up with those who have already achieved success. This is true anywhere, but in Japan it is even more important. Your professional associations and business contacts reflect directly on you. Native Japanese, or foreign Japanese with a good international education who come from a reputable family, will bring you much further than any expat. It is even better if they run their own business. You will never compete with them directly, so they will be able and willing to connect you.

Business Lesson

Instead of mingling with those who are also starting out like yourself, find people who are more successful than you. They rarely see you as a threat and will be in a position to help you advance your own goals with practical advice.

Use Your Credit While You Have It

Despite their long periods of isolation from the outside, the Japanese are a curious and innovative people. Whenever something is new, they want to know about it. No wonder that Japan is also the land of gadgets and fads. They create and export them, for example in form of comics, games, robots and animation. Some of them endure, others are a flash in the pan. Just think of *Pokemon*[4], *Tamagotchi*[5], or *Aibo*, the robot dog.[6]

As a newcomer, you have a window of opportunity where being unknown and different makes you interesting. When that short window has

---

[4] Wikipedia. Pokemon. http://en.wikipedia.org/wiki/Pok%C3%A9mon.
[5] Wikipedia. Tamagotchi. http://en.wikipedia.org/wiki/Tamagotchi.
[6] Wikipedia. Aibo. http://en.wikipedia.org/wiki/AIBO.

closed, your credit has expired. You will then have to try harder to get attention. When I came to Tokyo on my first business visit, I managed to see executives from several large record labels, film production companies and game producers. First meetings were surprisingly easy to land. We already learned that this was possible because of introductions through friends. However, the fact that I was working in Hollywood at the time, the entertainment capital of the world, helped as well. I got in the door this way, but then I had to deliver to stay there.

All the people you meet in new locations will generally be open and interested, and first meetings often end on a positive note. But when you try to see them again on your next visit, you will have to work harder. Your credit expires fast. Use it up while you can.

Business Lesson

You will have some initial credit when you are a newcomer in an industry or location, simply because nobody has heard of you. Make this window of opportunity count. You need to prove you are more than a novelty to keep the initial momentum alive.

Keep Your Guard Up

The Japanese like to organize their desks, drawers and closets just as much as they like to classify people. They do this by blood type, year of birth, or even by a system of character development from Japanese comics. Several manga character types exist, for example the following two:

- *Tsundere*: Describes a person who is initially cold or hostile towards another before gradually showing their warm side.[7]
- *Yandere*: A person who is initially kind, loving and caring before their admiration becomes mentally destructive, often through overprotectiveness or violence.[8]

With such detailed psychological profiles at their disposal, people you meet in Japan will inevitably analyze your actions and character. This is cute in a personal context, but when it comes to business, it can backfire. You should try to present yourself from your strongest side and should always

---

[7] Wikipedia. Tsundere (ツンデレ). http://en.wikipedia.org/wiki/Tsundere.

[8] Animanga Wiki. Yandere (ヤンデレ). http://animanga.wikia.com/wiki/Yandere.

come across as an expert. Even though someone may be friendly and personal, you should refrain from letting your guard down.

After he had a few drinks in him, I have a friend of mine admitted to a female Japanese co-worker that he was far less proficient in his field than he had made everybody believe. His confession promptly made the rounds in the company and landed him in hot water. Even when the atmosphere is friendly and personal after work, make sure you stay composed, and avoid getting drunk among your business peers (more on that later).

Studying one's behavior in a social context is a strength of the Japanese. Once they have assigned you a slightly negative or unreliable character type, it will be hard to shake that stigma. A good strategy is to go for "mysterious." When nobody can get a grip on what you are really thinking, you are generally safe.

Business Lesson

Even though things may seem personal after work hours, better keep your guard up. Avoid sharing details of professional or personal issues with your co-workers. They may match you with a negative stigma that will be hard to shake.

Arm Yourself With Stories

The Japanese have a reputation for being shy. Many of them are not that talkative, unless they have hoisted a few drinks. In a business context, it will often be up to you to entertain a whole group. It may be the language barrier or an innate insecurity that exists towards westerners. In any case, better prepare what you are going to do to avoid awkward silences.

Most Japanese have never left their country. If they did, they either studied abroad together with other Japanese exchange students, or they went on a packaged tour to a tourist destination. They may have been in Paris, London, New York, or Los Angeles for a few days, without ever leaving their Japanese group. Since their English is generally limited, a guide did all the talking with the locals. As a foreigner, you can contribute some interesting stories simply by telling them about life in your country. This topic is seldom something you would talk about with your friends or business partners elsewhere. Regardless, it goes a long way in Japan.

To gather some facts worth telling, look up your country and hometown on Wikipedia. Find out when they were founded, how many people live there, and other remarkable facts and figures about their origins and history.

Do the same with other interesting places you have been to, for example the place where you studied, or a recent journey. It also helps to put the numbers into context with Japan. Do you know how many people live in Los Angeles? Thirteen million. The same number of people live in Tokyo. But Los Angeles is twice as big. I also often talked about celebrities that I had sighted in the gym when I was working in Hollywood. Their extravagant beach houses also made for interesting stories.

Your own tales set the stage for questions to ask, and before you know it, you kick-started a lively conversation. Unless you prepare a few topics, you may find yourself at a loss when nobody else has anything to say. When you save the day by providing entertainment, you rise in the hierarchy of the group. This can only help when you try to establish yourself in a new place.

Business Lesson

Have a few conversation topics ready when you meet with a new group. If people are hesitant to talk, tell stories about your hometown, your country, or places you have visited. This may inspire others to join in the conversation. If nothing else, you saved the occasion from descending into dullness.

Speak in Glowing Terms About Your Home Country

Many expats have left their country for good when they emigrated to set up shop in a new location of their choice. Some are adventurers who left to try something new, others had no other choice and set out to destinations with better opportunities. Whatever their motivations, they all have a story to tell about their home country.

The Japanese love to take trips, both in their own territory and abroad. They often do this by traveling in groups where everything is organized for them. All they have to do is board a plane at Narita airport and sit back. Indeed a very convenient way to see the world. After their vacations, when they get the chance to talk with foreigners in Japan, they love to hear and share travel stories. Europe and America are exotic destinations for the Japanese. They collect tales about them and add them to their own memories from a past vacation.

This is the perfect chance for foreigners to build rapport when being new to Japan. However, what some foreigners tell the Japanese about their countries is often the exact opposite of what they want to hear. If someone left in anger, perhaps because he lost his job and had difficulty finding a new one, he complains about all the things he finds wrong with his country. How unfair the economic system has become, how the cost of living has shot through the roof, or how the place is going to hell in a hand basket. I have seen Japanese listen to such accounts in shock, especially about Europe. Europe as they know it is a dream destination with untouched nature, beautiful lakes, rich history and culture, elegant metropolises and exquisite food. It is a place they spend a lot of money to visit. When someone complains to them that France is overrun by African immigrants, England cares more about Russian oligarchs than its own people, or Germany is picking up the slack of all the lazy EU member states, their illusion shatters. Of course they read the paper and know what is going on in the world. Nevertheless, when they ask foreigners about their home countries, they want to hear glowing accounts of how beautiful they really are.

If you have issues with your home country, get over them as quickly as possible. When you build a new network abroad and get a chance to speak about the place you are coming from, focus on the positive points. Paint a beautiful picture and offer to tell more or show photos. Visit your embassy, they often have picture books available for free for their citizens. Pick up a few and gift them to your Japanese friends. When you give them the fairy tale version of your native land, you will impress them beyond measure.

Business Lesson

Paint a positive picture of your home country when you get a chance to talk about it. Awe-inspiring accounts of your exotic homeland give others something to dream about. This embeds you in their memory better and faster.

Make Wild Promises

Have you ever made a promise that you later found too hard to keep? If that happened, you may have concluded that you should refrain from making similar promises in the future. After all, we should only promise something that is within reach. Why would anybody be interested in it otherwise?

This is a limiting belief when you are in Japan. Nowhere else did I hear promises so outrageous. People I had just met offered to take me on sightseeing trips through Japan. When they learned I was interested in green tea, they volunteered to teach me the tea ceremony. At first business meetings, people professed that we would surely do many projects together in Japan. The list of promises goes on. The common thread is that none of them were easy to keep, and those who made them never followed up. It was obvious from the beginning that these promises were unrealistic. Nevertheless, it is what the Japanese do to establish a friendly rapport.

I experimented with this technique. When they mentioned they enjoyed snow, I would invite Japanese strangers to ski trips in the Alps. Were they interested in Los Angeles? We should all travel there together, rent a car and drive through California on Highway 1. If someone talked about music, I would propose we should produce an album or film score together. As expected, I got only positive reactions to my impossible promises. Nobody ever came back and asked when exactly we would go on that trip or produce music together. They understood it was just a friendly way to establish positive rapport.

Making empty promises is uncommon in the West. Conversations are supposed to be realistic and we take care to avoid extending ourselves too far. In Asia, this is different. Unless you make big promises to new acquaintances, they find you reserved and cold. Suggesting activities together is a form of small talk that shows your generosity. Luckily, following up is unnecessary.

Business Lesson

Experiment with making generous promises when you meet people for the first time. It immediately establishes an interesting conversation and strong rapport. Should they ask you to follow up, find a convenient excuse. Expect the same from others.

Be Aggressive, Passively

Foreigners often describe the Japanese as a docile, domesticated people. The women are passive, subordinate secretaries and homemakers, and the men sport handbags, put great pride in their hairstyles and look immature and sexless past the age of thirty. On the other end of the spectrum are the action heroes in manga and anime and the brave samurai in Japanese history dramas. Of course, all these perceptions are stereotypes that only hold at a cursory glance. There is much more depth to the Japanese when you look under the surface.

For example, it is the women who trade on the currency and equity markets in Japan. As the guardians of household savings, they move trillions of yen around the global financial system.[9] Husbands receive the paychecks, but their wives are in charge whenever money and investments are concerned. At home, Japanese women are anything but docile. The submissive female is mainly a convention they adopt outwardly.

It is true that modern Japanese men are less status-conscious than their fathers who lived through the boom-and-bust cycle of the 1980s and 90s. However, Japanese companies dominate the global economy in several sectors. Toyota is the world's largest auto maker, selling close to ten million cars per year.[10] Two Japanese banks, Mitsubishi UFJ Financial Group (MUFG) and Nomura, are in the group of fifty companies who exert disproportionate power over the world economy.[11] The country leads in the number of worldwide patent applications in the following fields: Electrical machinery, audio-visual technology, telecommunications, semiconductors, optics, measurement, control, marcomolecular chemistry, polymers, metallurgy, coating, environmental technology, mechanical engineering, furniture and games.[12] Despite their perceived passivity, Japan and its people have great influence in the world far beyond their own borders.

I was lucky to work with Japanese who were humble and unassuming outwardly, but extremely talented and brilliant in their fields. Judging a book by its cover did them no justice. Being underestimated often was to their advantage. They were far away from the spotlight and could pursue their goals through the backdoor without being a perceived threat. Japan achieved much of its global success this way. When the competition woke up to the fact that this small country controlled entire world markets, it was already too late do catch up.

---

[9] McLannahan, Ben; Ross, Alice. Ms Watanabe Comes Out of Hiding. Financial Times, March 11, 2013. http://www.ft.com/intl/cms/s/0/55e7c266-8a3a-11e2-9da4-00144feabdc0.html.

[10] Dawson, Chester. Toyota Again World's Largest Auto Maker. Wall Street Journal, January 28, 2013.
http://online.wsj.com/news/articles/SB10001424127887323375204578269181060493750.

[11] Coghlan, Andy; MacKenzie, Debora. The Capitalist Network That Runs the World. New Scientist, October 24, 2011.
http://www.newscientist.com/article/mg21228354.500-revealed--the-capitalist-network-that-runs-the-world.html

[12] World Intellectual Property Organization (WIPO). 2013 World Intellectual Property Indicators. http://www.wipo.int/ipstats/en/wipi/.

Business Lesson

Assume a passive and unassuming stance outwardly. Underneath the surface, push aggressively toward your goals. When nobody perceives you as a threat, they will only notice you surpassed them when it is already too late.

Use Clean Language

Japanese are polite and so is their language. Not only does it sound cute, there are also countless grammar rules for deference to superiors, expressing politeness and humility. Let's examine this with an example. When asking in English where to find chocolate in a supermarket, you would simply say: "Where is the chocolate?" In Japanese, you express the question in the following way: "Excuse me, you don't have chocolate, right?" You ask the shop staff indirectly and imply that you will not be disappointed if the supermarket is out of chocolate. Nevertheless, you still get what you want. This is just a simple example. The Japanese language is full of such twists and turns, with many ways of saying the same thing but different. Knowing which expression to choose in a particular situation often baffles even decade-long students.

On the other hand, English and other Western languages have seen a steady infiltration with slang and swearwords in recent years. Expressions involving expletives like s**t, f**k, a**hole and others fail to raise any eyebrows in America and Europe today. Softer diminutives, such as loser, idiot, or jerk, will not even register. Sure, the Japanese also know how to talk slang. However, if they do, they only use it in private among friends. They would never wield foul language in business, with their parents, or their superiors. When you speak with Japanese people, you need to adjust your vocabulary to avoid confusion and misunderstandings.

I had been recording in a studio outside of Tokyo and was driving back into the city in a taxi together with a singer. About halfway there I noticed that my backpack felt awfully light. I inspected it and found we had forgotten some magazines that I had brought to kill time at the studio. It was the singer who had taken them out without putting them back. Without thinking anything about it, I muttered the f-word. To my surprise, the singer clammed up, started whimpering softly, and then burst out into tears. "Please don't hate me," she stammered, crying bitterly. It was the saddest thing. These magazines were unimportant, and that word meant nothing. I was already tired from the studio day, and now I found myself in an hour-long cab ride with a bawling twenty-two-year-old, getting miserable myself.

Expletives were something I had picked up in Los Angeles. It took some effort to purge my vocabulary. This has been a big advantage since. Decision makers and successful professionals rarely use gutter language. If you want them to take you seriously, better avoid it as well.

Business Lesson

Avoid swearwords, gutter language and slang. It may be fine among your peers for a while, but decision makers and successful business people put much stock in a clean vocabulary. If you want them to take you seriously, better follow their example.

Avoid Self-made Obstacles

Before I started working with the record label in Tokyo, they flew me and my team from Los Angeles to Tokyo to work on the legal agreements. One of the Americans I brought with me had a tattoo of the kanji character *ai* (愛, "love") on his forearm. He did not speak or understand Japanese but was obviously proud of his tattoo. Unfortunately, only Yakuza and other delinquents openly display their tattoos in Japan. Some young people have small tattoos somewhere, but they hide them in public. In any case, being perceived as riff-raff does not inspire the respect and trust that you need to forge a strong professional relationship with an international business conglomerate. I therefore asked this guy to cover up the tattoo by wearing a long business shirt. He grudgingly agreed.

Fast forward a week. We are sitting around a table in a conference room in Tokyo, three westerners on one side, five Japanese in their fifties wearing tailored suits on the other side. The negotiations are going sluggishly. The Japanese say, "Why won't you just sign the contract!" This contract needs to come a long way before I am confident to sign it. That is the moment the American rolls up his sleeves. Unaware of it, his tattoo makes its entrance at the worst possible moment. Nobody says anything, but the faces of the Japanese speak volumes. The little ground we had gained is quickly lost. In the end, after several days of back and forth, the deal goes through, but much less elegantly than it could have.

I learned about this aversion to tattoos when I joined a gym in Tokyo. When I needed to fill out a questionnaire about my health, one question explicitly addressed them. That particular gym would only admit people without any tattoos, however small they were. When I asked for the reason, they said that they wanted to avoid gang members hanging out on their premises. Sure, some foreigners had tattoos without being in a gang, but some of the gym's older patrons would not be aware of that. They would feel that the gym was going down in status by admitting criminals and other undesirables.

Why are the Japanese so picky about this? Through the ages, the body has always been a sanctuary in Japan. What you do with it reflects on your personality and character. Even though it seems overly conservative, sporting tattoos, piercings and other body modifications are no small issue in some circles. Yes, there are punks in Harajuku with more piercings in their lips, ears and eyebrows than you can count. But are these your role models to achieve fame and fortune in business or as an entrepreneur? As a foreigner in Japan you already have enough preconceived notions to overcome. Better put up as few hurdles for yourself as possible.

Business Lesson

Body ornaments like tattoos, piercings, facial hair or extravagant hairstyles that are acceptable in some cultures may offend in others. Make things easy for yourself. Adopt a professional look and demeanor in business relationships or you will be up against obstacles that you put up yourself.

Look Presentable

Most Japanese are obsessed with cleanliness. Sure, you will also see some people with appalling personal hygiene in Japan, especially when you ride the subway during rush hour on a daily basis. They exist everywhere. Nevertheless, personal hygiene and the private homes of most Japanese are spotless. Some people carry with them disposable sheets they put on the seat in a taxi or subway to avoid contact with surfaces touched by others. Many wear gloves when touching the strap handles on the train. At the very minimum, if you have ever been in Tokyo, you will have noticed that every other person wears a surgical mask as a shield against germs and bacteria.

There is no need to be this extreme. But you should pay attention to your personal hygiene when you interact with Japanese. Your appearance should be clean or you will raise suspicions about your character. Men should shave daily. Another important thing to remember is that you need to take off your shoes when entering a private home. In some smaller offices, the same applies. Make sure your shoes and socks are clean. It sounds silly to say this, but more often than once have I seen a foreigner embarrassed when a Japanese host turned away when he took off his sneakers, or when his socks spotted large holes.

Most Japanese are too polite to tell you when you made a mistake. To double-check if you are in the clear, just look around and use common sense. If there are shoes outside a door, chances are you should take off yours as well. Nobody will remind you of the basic tenets of personal hygiene either. They may just not invite you back or give you another meeting, and you will never learn why. Japan is already difficult enough to do business in as a foreigner. Stack the deck in your favor by observing a few simple rules and using common sense.

Business Lesson

Make sure your clothes, shoes and socks are clean. In some countries, you may need to take them off (the shoes) in offices, homes, or restaurants. Spend a few minutes on neatness each day. This stacks the deck in your favor in a huge way.

Drink Without Drinking

Getting drunk is a welcome emotional outlet for the Japanese. It is common for office staff to go out drinking together after work hours, especially on Friday evenings. People tend to excuse whatever others may say or do under the influence of alcohol. This is often the only time they can voice their honest opinion or make jokes about the boss. The next day in the office, all of this is completely forgotten. Of course, there is a line that you should not cross. But you can go surprisingly far under the pretext that you were drunk and did not know what you were saying.

Alcohol does not agree with my body. I get unwell from one beer or half a glass of wine and do not particularly enjoy the feeling. In social situations I rarely drink, and if I do, it is very little. In my years in Tokyo, I could have joined drinking binges every other night. After the first few parties, I needed to come up with a strategy to cut down my intake. Otherwise, I would have gotten zero work done the entire time. I tried to refuse alcohol, only to be teased and talked into "bottoms up" even more. I tried to decline indirectly by saying I felt ill, only to be persuaded that this or that alcoholic drink would cure whatever ailed me.

The Japanese love making toasts, and when all you drink is bottled water, they feel slightly offended. When a group goes out together, they want everybody to participate in their rituals. Refusing to do so can make you an outsider fast. Especially when you build your network, you need others to accept you as a peer. In Japan, there is no way around joining people on their bar crawls, since they are a favorite pastime and a great opportunity to analyze others in a less formal setting. I finally happened upon a technique that worked well. Everybody thought I was drinking but I was not. Here's how it works.

When I joined others on a night out in Japan, I made sure people would see me order a Jack and Coke or gin tonic and toasted with everybody. Without drinking anything, I would "forget" that drink about fifteen minutes into the evening on a table somewhere and swap it with a similar looking non-alcoholic beverage. Diet Coke looks like Jack and Coke when you put ice and a straw in it. Soda water passes as a gin tonic with enough slices of lime. This is what I was drinking for the rest of the evening, and nobody was any the wiser. Pretending to drink alcohol sounds silly, I know. But if you are like me and do not take well to it, this trick can be a lifesaver. I was a member of the group for the night and would wake up fresh as a daisy the next day. The added advantage was that I had a clear head to study the social dynamics of the groups I went out with. As soon as they felt they could speak their mind under the cloak of alcohol, it was quite obvious who were the informal leaders and who had a weak standing. Staying sober helped me notice the nuances.

Business Lesson

If you must go out drinking in bars with others to strengthen your professional network, cut down your alcohol intake. Swap your drink with a similar looking non-alcoholic beverage. You can participate in toasts and observe the hierarchy of the group while keeping a clear head.

Putting Others Down - The Japanese Way

Putting others down is a form of banter, an art that many Japanese have mastered. Making fun of people in a playful way is part of other cultures as well, but they take it one step further: It is perfectly fine to aim way below the belt. What may seem harsh and downright mean to foreigners is a source of great laughter among the Japanese, including the person who is the center of the joke.

I was having a meeting with two Tokyo businessmen who had known each other since their college days. They had both studied in America and were now in their fifties. One of them owned a software company that supplied the government, the other one was a professional yacht racer. After they had hoisted a few, things became lively. I asked about how they had started out in business and the yacht racer started telling his friend's story. It went like this.

"He had always been stupid, already in college in Boston. Only the ugly girls would go out with him. I was ashamed to be his friend and told nobody that I knew him. After we graduated, his father wanted him to work in his construction company in Tokyo. The old man is a Yakuza (Japanese mafia), you know. But this guy refused to come home to Japan. He missed the flight and stayed in New York. He even managed to marry a blonde American woman; I think he paid her a lot that she agreed. But then his old man threatened to cut him off and stopped sending money. And what did this stupid guy do? He folded right away. Divorced his wife and came back to Japan, tail between his legs. Yakuza don't need to kill anymore, they do everything with money now. When he came back to Japan, they arranged a marriage for him, and he started to work in the construction company. But he was so bad at it, that his father was happy to let him go and gave him money to start his own firm. So he did, and through his Yakuza connections, his dad got him some government deals. That's how he set himself up in business."

I sat there flabbergasted. Both men were howling with laughter all the way through the story. The yacht racer did not pull any punches and the software company owner did not seem to mind. He laughed along with every joke. I have known him for almost ten years now. When I asked him if his father really was a Yakuza, he said yes. He had done a shoddy job in the construction company to distance himself from his family. I asked if the rest of the story was true. He said it was, more or less. The yacht racer was like an older brother, he explained, and it was perfectly OK for him to talk this way.

This was a fascinating evening. It was the finest comedy you could imagine. However, stay out of this yourself. The unspoken hierarchies that allow someone to put another down are impossible to know. I have found some Japanese to be extremely touchy when I made harmless jokes at the expense of others, so I have since stayed off this thin ice in business conversations, both in Japan and elsewhere.

Business Lesson

Refrain from putting others down, in earnest and in jokes. You may cross a line without noticing it. When you see others in this kind of banter, there may be an unspoken hierarchy that allows them to hit below the belt. Unless you understand the pecking order, better make safe jokes in business.

Adjust Your Speech Pattern and Pretend to Understand

Even though most Japanese people speak some English, their proficiency is modest. Unless they have lived and studied abroad for several years, they will be better at grammar and theory than conversation. Their reading and writing may be advanced, but when they speak, their lack of experience shows. Foreigners find it hard to understand the heavily accented English of the Japanese. Likewise, those with English as their mother tongue have a hard time to be understood. Their speech is often too fast and colored with an American, British or Australian accent. For them, communication in Japan turns out to be frustrating.

Nevertheless, being a non-native English speaker is an advantage in Japan. I was used to speaking slow with those who had a hard time understanding me, and I had no reservations to mangle the language or to speak with a mock Japanese accent. When I needed to find out the location of the train station, I simply asked: "Train, where?" This is how you would phrase the question in Japanese. A native English speaker might naturally say: "Pardon me, but you wouldn't happen to know where the station is, would you?" They often feel silly when they need to dumb down their language. The result is that their conversations, especially with Asians, go nowhere.

The same applies to listening to the Japanese when they speak to you. They may believe their English is excellent, but you will hardly understand what they try to say. Especially when they make jokes or use figures of speech, you often need to turn their words around in your head a few times to solve the puzzle. That they mix up the phonetics of "R" and "L" makes things even more cryptic. Just as a Japanese person to pronounce the word "incredible." Instead of honestly trying to understand their words, I often just went along with the reaction of the majority. When something was supposed to be funny, I laughed. When they tried to explain something to me, I would nod my head and say that I understood. Most of the time, it was less important to grasp their every word than to keep the good mood intact and the conversation going.

Business Lesson

When others feel you speak the same language and understand them, making friends is easy. Mirror their speech patterns and use the same words they do. If you struggle to understand something they try to say, act as if you did. If it is critical, you can still clarify later.

Learn to Say "No" Without Speaking a Word of Japanese

Even though there are words in the Japanese dictionary to express "no," you usually tiptoe around an issue instead of turning it down flat out. The easiest strategy is simply to accept everything and later find a way out. For example, you should always accept invitations. Do you want to go to the zoo on Sunday with a business partner, his wife and his kids? Sure. Come Friday, you simply call and say you need to work over the weekend. However, when an action is immediate, you need a different strategy. Here is one that a Japanese friend taught me.

Many Japanese drink green tea on a daily basis. Coffee has made inroads, especially since there is a Starbucks or similar franchise on every street corner in every major city, but traditional Japanese prefer to drink tea. Not just any tea, but high-quality *Japanese* green tea, prepared in the right way. As you can imagine, this is not exactly a staple in the standard coffee shop. The green tea bags available at Starbucks and its cohorts are usually filled with substandard green tea from India or China. Since it is increasingly common to have business meetings at a coffee chain, my friend needed to come up with a strategy to decline coffee when she was asked if she wanted one. She found an elegant Japanese solution. "Can I get you a coffee?" someone would inquire, to which she responded: "Thank you, perhaps next time. I'm not thirsty right now." This is an exact translation of how you would decline something in Japanese. Instead of directly refusing, you would say: "It's OK. Please ask me again next time." When next time comes around, you give the same answer again. And so it goes, round and round.

A direct rebuff comes across as being harsh and ungrateful in Japan. You should refrain from saying that you dislike something, especially certain foods. If you say you hate a dish that turns out to be a specialty in your host's province, you will alienate him for sure. Better use the Japanese strategy or indirect rejection. "Next time," works well. So does "I'm not hungry/thirsty right now."

Business Lesson

You need to say "no" sometimes. A direct rebuff may hurt someone's feelings. Find creative ways to turn down offers politely. Using indirect language and ambiguity makes you look sophisticated and mindful.

How to Deal With Blunders

You may have read all the books you could find about Japanese etiquette. You may have asked your Japanese friends how to behave in this and that situation. And you may have practiced bowing or giving business cards in front of the mirror. Inevitably, you will find yourself committing blunders in Japan where you wished the ground would open and swallow you up. Even the Japanese sometimes use the wrong words to address a superior. They may turn the tea cup in the wrong direction in the tea ceremony or make another gaffe that does not even register with the uninitiated. Mistakes happen to the best of us.

In a culture so rich with rules and protocol as Japan, get used to making blunders. Instead of being nervous trying to do everything the right way, draw the line and relax. Nobody expects you to be Japanese, after all. Learn the basics of greeting and using chopsticks, and then go with the flow. You can pick up additional customs and rules on the fly. When you do make a mistake, remain polite and apologize. Smile, fix the situation as good as you can, and then act normal as if nothing happened. This is how the Japanese deal with their own blunders. Unless you want to make things more complicated than they are, do the same.

Business Lesson

Get used to making mistakes from time to time. When they occur, be polite, apologize and correct the situation. Then act as if nothing happened.

ATOM ALEX HELLING

CHAPTER 3: BUSINESS MEETINGS

Business meetings have much in common with the techniques we learned in the chapter about networking and communication. Most of them apply here as well, particularly when you meet people for the first time. This chapter explains the proper protocol to start meetings with the greeting and business card ritual and adds some strategies that are particularly useful in second meetings. They help you to deepen the relationship when you already know the other party and are ready to speak about projects in more detail in meetings at their office.

Greeting Protocol

In the West, it is customary to shake hands when meeting others formally. Privately, we often hug and kiss our friends when we see them. None of this is customary in Japan, where business greetings consist of a stiff bow. Saying hello to friends often follows the same protocol. Lovers rarely hold hands in public, let alone kiss or hug. Understanding how to greet people properly is the bare minimum you should know about Japanese customs.

When they meet with foreigners, some Japanese will shake hands. However, some people are afraid of germs and believe touching others is a health hazard. To be safe, unless a person takes the initiative and extends his hand to shake yours, refrain from making the first move. It may end up in an embarrassing wet-noodle handshake, which is rarely a good starting point for a business meeting.

Men bow in a different way from women. They press their hands on their sides, stiffen their upper body and then bend it forward while looking the other person in the eyes. Women fold their hands in front of their bodies and then bow. How deep you bow depends on who you meet. Whoever bows deeper is lower in status than the other person. If you meet an equal, then just bow slightly or only nod your head. When you meet children, perhaps those of a business partner at his home, then you need not bow at all. Just wave, say hello, or make a victory sign.

In my music project, a manager from Los Angeles had joined me for meetings in Tokyo. He had never been to Japan and was eager to visit for the first time. We would also meet the families of some of my business partners there, so there were both business meetings and private get-togethers on the agenda. The Californian way of social conduct could hardly be more different from the rigid rules in Japan. LA is one of the most informal places that I know when it comes to business etiquette. On top of that, the manager from Los Angeles was a hugger. He would greet people hugging them with both arms, sometimes giving them a slap on the back while doing so. This may have been charming in the music business in

Hollywood but not so in Tokyo.

Knowing this, I instructed him of how things work in Japan. I even forwarded a short article to him outlining the proper way to greet others respectfully. The matter was then closed in my mind. I am no micromanager, and this guy was a grown-up. Everything went well in the business meetings. But when we met in a more private setting, he reverted back to his hugging ways. With a few drinks in him, he hugged the teenage sister of one my business partners and did the same with someone's mother. Their faces expressed sheer terror, which he failed to notice. It took a lot of explaining on my part that this was standard custom in America and in Los Angeles in particular. But when someone violates the personal space of others, you can patch up only so much with words. Needless to say that this was his first and last trip to Japan in my project. If you are serious about business in Japan, better not be this guy.

Business Lesson

Adjust the way you say hello and introduce yourself to local customs. Beware of invading the personal space of strangers. Especially in Asia, you should avoid shaking hands, hugs and kisses. Just watch what the locals do and mirror them.

Business Cards

That business cards are necessary when networking and meeting people is a no-brainer. Still, many newcomers forget to plan ahead and show without them in a new place. I have seen expats at networking events who scribbled down their phone numbers on napkins. Especially in Asia, this makes a poor impression. Most school children already have business cards and so should any new arrival to a new industry or location.

When you work at a company, they will print cards for you. However, it may take several weeks until they are ready, so you may end up empty-handed in the first weeks after your arrival. If you are student or researcher at a university, avoid giving people the card from your university. Better print your own at a professional copy center. For entrepreneurs, there are a few standard rules for business cards. They should include:

- Your name and degree, for example Dr. X, MBA;
- Your title at the company, for example CEO;

- The name of the company;

- The address of your primary place of business. If you just moved to a city, then put the address of the place where you are staying (hotel or apartment).

- Your personal mobile phone number. Get a local number as soon as possible.

- Your personal email address. Get your own dot-com domain for your startup at a domain hoster like Godaddy.com. This costs about fifteen dollars per year and comes with free email accounts. Setting up your page and email address takes ten minutes. This looks infinitely better than a faculty email or free Gmail address.

Your title is important. First time entrepreneurs are often unsure about their role in their company. Are they the founder, the CEO (chief executive officer), the Chief Scientist, or all of the above? In any case, avoid using the title of "founder." If you are the boss of your team, then write CEO, or managing director, or president. If you are working in the background, then put CTO (chief technical officer), or CIO (chief information officer) on your card. Briefly read up on these abbreviations on Wikipedia and then choose the one that fits best what you are doing. Only use one title, even if you have several roles.

In Asia, one side of the card should be in English, the other side in the native language. The Japanese use three different alphabets: *Kanji* (漢字) for formal and academic writing, *hiragana* (ひらがな) for informal writing, and *katakana* (カタカナ) for writing foreign words and names. *Katakana* is the one you should use. Have a friend translate your name for you or feel free to contact me through my website (information at the end of this book) and I will send you the translation for your name.

When you meet people in Japan, hold your card in front of you with both hands and then pass it to the other person with a slight bow. When receiving a card from a Japanese person, stare at it for five seconds while nodding your head. Ask for the other person's name if you need clarification, since they normally put their family name in front of their given name. The business card counts as an extension of a person, so by studying it, you pay your respects and acknowledge their presence. In a meeting, keep all the cards you receive in front of you on the table. Wait until the end of the meeting to put them away. Putting them in the back pocket of your pants is bad etiquette. Better get a small card case to you store them. Also avoid writing on someone's card in their presence. And finally, it goes without saying that you should not refuse cards. All of this may sound more complicated than it is. After you have seen the Japanese exchange cards a couple of times, you will know how it works.

Business Lesson

Create professional business cards if you are self-employed or looking for work. Your card says a lot about your personality. Also study the cards you receive from others. You may get some insight what it will be like working with them in the future.

Giving and Receiving Presents

You should bring a small present when you have meetings with business people at their office in Japan. As a foreigner, something related to your home country always works well. There is no need to go overboard: As long as it tells a story and shows that you care, you are in the clear. A photo book or edible delicacies are usually safe. If you stay longer in Japan, make sure you visit your embassy in Tokyo. If you are lucky, they have picture books available for free for their citizens. Take a few with you and gift them to your Japanese business contacts. Otherwise, spending somewhere in the neighborhood of twenty dollars if acceptable. Wrap your gifts or place them in a gift bag. When you buy something in Japan, ask if they can wrap it for you.

Most of the time, your Japanese host will have a present for you as well. This is usually a local pastry or cake, a Japanese tea cup, or another traditional Japanese item. Remember that gifts are normally opened in private. You should refrain from unwrapping your presents in the meeting and prepare yourself that your host will do the same. The reason for this is that people want to avoid embarrassment if one of the gifts differs widely from the other. If you receive a gold coin when all you gave your host is a free book from the embassy, this would be such an occasion.

The right moment to exchange presents is at the beginning of the meeting. Hold back until after the greeting and business card ritual. If the occasion feels right, you may present your gift to the host now. Otherwise, wait until the host to has made a brief introduction to the meeting and has given his gift to you. Rules for presents are much less strict in other countries, especially in the West. However, when you think about your host and bring them a little token of appreciation from abroad, you always gain a few extra points.

Business Lesson

A gift establishes goodwill in your favor. Just as you should never show up empty-handed when invited at somebody's home, bringing a small token of appreciation to a business meeting goes a long way.

The Right Sequence

As long as you show respect and interest to learn, the Japanese can be very forgiving if you are unaware how to deal with proper etiquette and protocol. To save you from harm, they will often assist you in any way possible.

Assume you entered the office of your Japanese host. You bowed, presented your business card and handed over your present. Now it is time to progress to the conference room and start the meeting. But there are still some hurdles ahead. One of them is the sequence of events when sitting down around the conference table. The seating order is very important in Japan, since it reflects the status of people in a company. The highest ranking person will take the seat at the head of the table closest to the entrance. Higher ranking people will sit closer to the head, and their importance gradually decreases toward the opposite side of the table. Instead of plunking down at the nearest available chair, best wait for direction where to sit.

As a rule, you should avoid being the first one sitting down. Look around you first: When people start taking their seats, do the same. The same goes with any other action during the meeting, such as speaking, drinking and eating. When your host offers you something to drink, wait until everybody has their beverage in front of them and then wait for the most important person to take a sip first. This is also important outside the workplace, for example in restaurants. Wait until your host or superior makes the first move, then follow. When Japanese see you behave this way, you immediately rise in their graces. Good manners count, both in the workplace and in private relations. Call this old-fashioned, but that's how things are in Japan.

Business Lesson

In some cultures, you should wait with doing anything before those of higher status have done it. Sequence reflects the hierarchy in a group. You can bend the rules a little bit as long as you show you know them. Good manners, even if you consider them old-fashioned, go a long way.

Read Between the Lines

When we talked about politely declining offers in the indirect Japanese way, we looked at things from our own perspective. We were the ones who wanted to get out of a situation without offending anyone. On the same token, others may need to refuse us a favor and will do so in the most indirect way imaginable. They may be so good at it that we fail to recognize their true intentions. We believe they really are not in the mood right now, have already eaten, or that we should please ask them soon again. Unless you know the hidden meaning of these words, they are easy to misinterpret.

You can always ask others to help you, but observe their reactions with care. To avoid ending up in an endless loop of polite rejection, learn to read between the lines in Japan. Look at people's body language, their facial expression, and learn to recognize the indirect words they use to tell you something. Listen to your gut feeling as well. When you are only listening to their words, you will miss most of the conversation. *How* people say something and in which context is often more important. Especially in Japan, where indirectness and deference were invented, this skill is valuable. Master it as early as possible. When in doubt, ask friends how to interpret a particular situation. You may be surprised how they analyze it in ways you never imagined.

Business Lesson

Instead of relying only on the words people write or say, read between the lines. Facial expression, body language, tone of voice, timing and context often give away all the information you need to know.

Mirror Others

Once you start digging, you will uncover layer upon layer of rules that are impossible to memorize in Japan. Instead of trying to master them, better make it a habit to mirror what your Japanese counterparts are doing. Find someone who is roughly your equal in status and age and then copy what he or she is doing. This is a simple strategy that can save much headache. Mirroring makes everything easy.

When you experience your first tea ceremony in Japan, you will know what I mean. The host of the ceremony often goes to great lengths to prepare, practicing movements of their hands and the steps of the ceremony for years before they are perfect. The tea ceremony often takes place in a special tea room, adorned with Japanese scrolls and flower arrangements (*ikebana*). Guests may have to wait in a waiting room until the host is ready to receive them. This room is sometimes separated by a patch of grass from the tea room. Walking across the grass symbolizes purification from worldly matters before the ceremony. You will also wash your hands and mouth with water from some kind of stone basin to purify your body before entering the tea room.

Most of the ceremony is silent. Communication mainly exists in the form of different bows and gestures. The first step of the ceremony is cleaning and preparing the utensils necessary for the preparation of the tea. This takes place in front of the guests. The host then adds green tea powder to a tea bowl, adds water, and whips it into a bubbly paste with a bamboo whisk before adding more water. This can take anywhere between five and fifteen minutes. The host then presents the prepared bowl to one of the guests and they exchange bows. The guest admires the bowl and rotates it several times in different directions before taking a small sip. All guests usually share one bowl, and they wipe its rim before passing it to the next person. Drinking the tea takes about ten minutes. After cleaning the empty bowl and utensils, the guests inspect the tools used in the ceremony. Some of them are passed down in families through generations, and they are valuable and delicate. You may need to use a special cloth to touch them. After the inspection, guests exit and complete the ceremony with a bow.

Experiencing a tea ceremony in Japan is about more than drinking green tea. It is about being part of an ancient tradition, a privilege that foreigners have not had for centuries. There are different kinds of tea ceremonies. The one I just described is what I experienced in Kyoto. When you travel on your own, you will rarely have access to this kind of experience. If a group of Japanese invites you, then tag along and mirror what everybody else is doing. As you might imagine, the potential to make mistakes always looms. When you care about doing things right, you will enjoy the experience much more. It is the real thing. This is much easier when you simply let a local go ahead of you and then follow in their footsteps.

Business Lesson

There is often no need to memorize complex protocols when you are in the company of others. Precisely watch and mirror what they do to avoid mistakes.

Toot Your Horn Smartly

Despite the fact that Japan is the land of humility and deference, you still need to tell others about your accomplishments. A job well done no longer speaks for itself. You must demonstrate what others gain from working with you before there is a project. Unless you toot your horn, there is no music. Nevertheless, there is a fine line in bragging. It is easy to get carried away and toot your horn too loudly. Less is more, and you should learn to do it in a smart way.

The best advertising is always someone else who does the bragging for you. Indirectly broadcasting your status fits well with the Japanese mentality. If you can show magazines with interviews you gave, articles you published or other highly visible proofs of your awesomeness, then bring them along. When you are in a meeting with a group, then have someone introduce you in the most glowing terms. Remember, Japanese love foreigners who have achieved success elsewhere. When they come to their country to show them how it is done, doors slide open.

You may have run a successful business without media attention or other prestigious trophies to show for it. But what about your client list? Make a print and bring it along. Do you have sales statistics? Japanese are adept at dealing with abstract data, so you may want to bring a pie chart of the market share your company achieved. In any case, it pays to prepare your collateral before you arrive in Japan. When you know you go there, begin to snap pictures of happy customers, get statements and testimonials from them, and start collecting anything else you can use to show your expertise and success.

Just saying that you are the best without proof will backfire in Japan. Let pictures, graphs and numbers to the talking for you. This also helps the Japanese present your case to their superiors. The data you give them to back up your story is their insurance policy. They avoid sticking out their neck, and when something goes wrong, they can point to the data and the fact that it looks flawless. As with most of the business lessons in this book, look at situations from the viewpoint of the Japanese. If you understand where they are coming from, it will be much easier for you to establish rapport and prosperous business relationships with them.

Business Lesson

Brag indirectly. Let published media articles, photos, graphs and numbers impress others. Social proof is powerful. It serves as an insurance policy for others when they recommend you.

CHAPTER 4: THE BUSINESS LUNCH OR DINNER

Food is extremely important in Japan, so it is no wonder that it also plays a big part in business relationships. Those who work together must also bond outside the office, and that is where drinking and sharing a meal comes in. How the Japanese view business lunches and dinners is distinctly different from the West. Eating together is rarely the first point of contact in Japan. You need to gain trust first and lay the groundwork for a professional relationship. Then your host will invite you out to see what kind of person you are privately. This chapter explains some of the observations I made eating with the Japanese and what I learned from them.

Focus on Food, Not Business

In *Business Lessons from Hollywood* I described how a business lunch in Los Angeles takes place. To make the most of it, you should be focusing first and foremost on business, not lunch. In Japan, things work the other way around: Food is something to look forward to and savor. How you do this tells the host something about your personality. You should therefore keep business talk out of casual lunches and dinners with your Japanese business partners.

Most of the time, the Japanese like to drink beer during meals. Whenever alcohol flows, business takes the backseat and it is time to relax. Keep things light, talk about your family or recent experiences you made during a vacation. Also ask your business partners about their private lives. They will happily tell you about their children, their hobbies and recent trips. When I asked if he had any pets at home, one guy pulled out a photo album with pictures of his purebred poodles. He took them to competitions and was quite successful, which he proved with another photo album of the trophies they had won. These are the kinds of topics that reign supreme in Japanese business lunches and dinners. Save the more professional matters for afterwards.

Business Lesson

In most countries, business lunches are just meetings outside the office. But some cultures frown upon talking about professional matters while eating. They rather hear about your personal stories and like to tell theirs. Adjust accordingly.

Reciprocate Immediately

Imagine you just ate a great meal together with a potential Japanese business partner. You learned a great deal about culture and customs and you both discussed your personal lives and viewpoints. Assume your host picked up the check, and the both of you are leaving the restaurant. Now you can do one thing that massively potentiates the impact of this meeting: Invite your host back immediately. You can do this by suggesting to get a coffee, dessert or drink at a nearby place right after leaving the restaurant. Let your host pick a place and then continue the meeting there. Until I discovered this, most lunch and dinner meetings would fizzle out towards then end, and everybody went their separate ways. Extending the meeting by inviting the other party made all the difference. It would keep people engaged and ended a lively evening on a high note.

Countless restaurants exist in Japan, and most of them specialize in one kind of food. A ramen shop or a sushi place will not serve anything else than what they are best known for. They may have a limited desert menu, but they will definitely not serve coffee or mixed drinks. Because most places are small, you should clear out of there relatively soon after finishing the meal to make room for the next wave of guests. Continuing the meeting in a coffee place or bar signals to your host that you found the conversation interesting. You would like to continue it and show your gratitude by inviting him or her in return. To do this in style, make sure you bring enough cash with you. Many smaller desert places and bars only accept paper money.

This extended part of the meeting is where you can carefully tiptoe back into some of the business questions you may have. Now the focus shifts away from what you are eating or drinking. Many times, people came forward with interesting propositions over a coffee or drink *after* the actual lunch or dinner meeting. I have since done this everywhere I go with excellent results.

Business Lesson

When your host invites you for a meal, invite him or her afterwards for coffee, desert, or a drink. You can express your gratitude and can bring the focus back to business matters in this extended part of the meeting.

Choice of Restaurant

When your Japanese hosts ask you where you would like to eat, let them decide. Like many things in Japan, this question is rhetorical in the first place. The Japanese often want to impress their guests, so they might have done research about a new restaurant and already made a reservation at a place to surprise you.

Not knowing any better, I have seen foreigners choose the worst restaurants and ruin the plans of their Japanese hosts without noticing it. An American I know asked his host to take him to a restaurant in Tokyo where he could eat a New York strip steak. Needless to say, the host had no idea what that was or where to find it. This made him look ignorant and he felt like he disappointed his guest. This is how the Japanese think. Most foreigners will not notice the embarrassment they are causing with unimportant requests. However, they may later complain that doing business in Japan is impossible. In most instances it is them who are to blame.

Others try to play it safe and mention that they would like to eat sushi. Your host may oblige and make it look like this is exactly what he or she had in mind. However, for a business meal, a Japanese host will hesitate to take you to a sushi place that serves food on a conveyor belt. Raw fish is a celebratory and expensive food that the Japanese rarely eat. The bill for a small party can amount to five hundred dollars or more. To put it another way: There is no good answer to the question where or what you would like to eat in Japan other than giving the question right back. Avoid ruining your host's plans for the meal. This is embarrassing for all parties and not a good start for a good business relationship.

When it is up to you to host someone in Japan, do your homework first. Find a place that is reasonable and quiet enough to have a personal conversation. There is no need to take your guests to a fancy place that costs hundreds of dollars for a simple lunch. You will find an original Japanese restaurant by asking around. Ethnic Asian food is good, such as Indian or Chinese. Italian food is also safe. Steak places are hit or miss in Japan, and they are usually expensive for what they offer. Better stay away from restaurants in Hotels. When you entertain younger people on a budget, American fast-casual food is popular, for example TGI Friday's, or a coffeehouse that also serves Japanese food.

As always, think from the perspective of the other person. If you are new to a country or city, let the host decide. This makes him look competent and gives him the chance to display good taste and savvy in choosing an interesting restaurant.

Business Lesson

If you are new to a country, let your host suggest a restaurant for a business meal. He may ask you where you would like to eat, but this question is rhetorical. When it is up to you to host guests, do your homework. Find a reasonable place that offers an interesting and relaxing experience.

Choice of Food

When you are a guest in Japan, unless you have allergies or a strong aversion towards certain foods, let your host pick something for you from the menu. Most of the time, it is written in Japanese anyway. The cuisine is extremely diverse and every region has its own specialties. Foreigners only know a fragment of bastardized dishes, such as California roll, that rarely do it any justice. When it is time to order food, best ask what your host recommends, keep an open mind, and brace yourself for an interesting experience.

    I had been invited by a business partner to join a small group for dinner at a Japanese restaurant in the Ginza district in Tokyo. The restaurant we went to looked very simple. Through an unassuming entry hall, a woman dressed in a Japanese kimono led our party of six to a private room. There was nothing in the room but a low table and seat cushions. I had not known the host for very long, so I felt honored to join his group to a traditional restaurant. He was the only person who was more or less fluent in English, so most of the conversation took place between him and me, and he translated to the rest of the group.

    There were no menus and I did not recall that anyone had placed an order because the server was nowhere to be seen. Out of nowhere, the first course arrived. It was a large plate with slices of raw fish (*sashimi*), arranged like a flower. It was delicious. The second course, a stew (*nabe*) made with vegetables and fish, also tasted excellent. Several dishes with fried fish and things I had trouble to identify followed. They all tasted amazing. The meal was a ceremony that lasted two hours. Towards the end, the host asked me if I knew what we had just eaten. Of course I had no idea. All five Japanese were giggling on the quiet. The host asked me if I had ever heard of blowfish (*fugu*). The whole meal had consisted of it.

    Sure I knew what blowfish was. Eating it is said to be the gastronomic equivalent of playing Russian roulette. Some of its body parts contain a poison so powerful that just a trace can kill a human in minutes. When I later looked it up in more detail, I learned that only specially licensed chefs may remove the poisoned organs of the fugu. These must be kept under lock and key and disposed of like plutonium waste in a special incinerator. Restaurants serve fugu sashimi in the shape of chrysanthemum, a traditional funeral flower.[13] Despite the slightly morbid overtones, this meal is still one of the best I ever ate in Japan.

Business Lesson

Let the host choose food for you if you are new to a foreign country. You may make an interesting experience. If you invite others and order for them, pick something that is easy to eat and has an interesting story.

Picking Up the Check

When business partners take you out for a meal in Japan, they will most likely invite you the first time around. Etiquette demands that a host treat his guests when they visit his country. It is safe to assume that your host will pick up the check. Just thank him and mention that you enjoyed the meal very much. If you reciprocate immediately afterwards, as we discussed earlier, by taking your host to a desert place or a bar, then you are usually square. There is no need to feel you need to pick up the check for the whole group at the next meal. Unless you are a heavy-hitter or doing business on a large scale, this would be overkill. By the way, tipping is uncommon in Japan. They may have a line that says "tip" on a credit card slip, but everybody leaves this empty.

If you host a group of Japanese people, then act in the same way as they would. Invite them for the first meal and then see if they reciprocate. Inviting them once is good manners. Doing it twice is unnecessary. After you have already gone out with people a few times, offer to split the check. Be aware that many restaurants in Japan, especially those outside the large cities, only accept paper money, so make sure you have enough cash with you. Put down your share of the bill and you are good to go.

---

[13] Facts and Details. Fugu in Japan.
http://factsanddetails.com/japan/cat19/sub123/item649.html.

Business Lesson

If you host, invite your guests the first time and see if they reciprocate. If you are the guest, your host will pick up the check the first time around. Reciprocating immediately by inviting them for coffee, desert, or drinks is enough. In future meals, pay your share with cash.

CHAPTER 5: DEAL-MAKING

When you have succeeded in making friends and business contacts in Japan and are ready to start a project, you need to seal the deal with a formal agreement. As you may expect, this is done quite differently from what you may be used to. The Japanese see contracts in a different light than Western business people.

Of course, when you deal with legal paperwork, you should hire a qualified lawyer. This chapter is no substitute for legal advice. On top of that, many books cover the ins and outs of selling your services, and explaining negotiation tactics in more detail is beyond the scope of this book.

Some of the lessons in this chapter may sound harsh. I am far from implying that the Japanese are a lawless people, or that they break their word. On the other hand, you must understand how to take care of your legal contracts so you are on the same page like your business partners. This includes knowledge of potential pitfalls and foul play. The lessons in this chapter give you hints how to come out on top. We will look at some of the situations with deal negotiation I encountered in Japan and the lessons I learned from them.

Reality Will Be Different

When I signed my deal with one of the largest Japanese record labels, an attorney from Los Angeles negotiated on my behalf. He and his staff were surprised how accommodating the Japanese and their legal team had been. The entire contract amounted to little more than fifty pages. For a seven-figure project, this is unheard-of in America or in Europe. It was almost too good to be true and it turned out it was.

We were in for an awakening when the project started. A few months in, things became complicated. Out of the blue, the Japanese asked us to transfer worldwide publishing rights to them at no cost. In music, these rights are about the most valuable asset that artists have. When I pointed out that we should negotiate a fair price, they retorted with the standard answer I would hear many more times in the months to come: "We never pay for publishing. This is how we do things in Japan." My business partner and me refused to give in, and they started stalling on their end. Their logic was the following: They accommodated us in the negotiation phase with preferential terms, and now it was up to us to play ball.

The way I see it, a legal contract in Japan is little more than a loose agreement to work on a project together. Most of the things that really matter will be discussed afterwards informally, based on how much goodwill you established, regardless what may be written in the contract.

Clinging to the deal terms will bode ill for a project, and the Japanese have ways to make it fizzle out if they want to. That is exactly what happened in my case. The label claimed that – regrettably – they had to re-allocate their resources. This left us with us two options: Sue them in a Japanese court, or renegotiate. Good luck trying to win as a party of two against one of the best-connected multinationals in Japan. This is where I left the project and my Japanese partner took over. She renegotiated, which spelled the beginning of the end. The project later disintegrated entirely, all the while hobbling along on empty promises by the record label. Even though the project was lucrative, I would think twice before doing such a deal again. But such is life, and that is another story altogether.

In some cultures, contracts may say one thing, but at the end of the day, everything is open for negotiation. Unless you know this and mentally prepare yourself, you will awaken halfway through the project when it is too late to change direction.

Business Lesson

> *A signed contract is no guarantee that your counterparty will stick to the deal terms. Everything may be different than outlined in the agreement. Think beforehand what you will do if this happens. The contract may be too expensive to enforce, so you need alternative strategies to manage your project.*

The Meaning of Contracts

As soon as you stop seeing contracts as legal instruments to specify every last detail in a project, you will have a more realistic idea how they work in Japan. In the Japanese business context, I see the function of a legal contract between business partners as the following:

- An agreement to work in mutual dependency on a particular project.
- A basis for renegotiation and making concessions.
- A means of control to show who is of higher status in the corporate hierarchy.

Rigid legal contracts are sharply at odds with the Japanese philosophy of *wa*, which means harmony in personal and professional relationships. Loyalty and consensus with the group in the long term are the most important thing in business relationships. American or European attorneys may not understand that. There will be a gulf between what they expect from a contract and how the Japanese view it. This can lead to endless negotiations and to projects that look great on paper but go nowhere in reality.

The terms of the deal also function as bargaining chips when the time comes to renegotiate. You can give up certain privileges that the other party promised in order to establish goodwill. Of course, this also works in the other direction. When your counterparty fails to deliver on promises, you can point out that they are breaking the harmony initially established in the project. All of this is a delicate dance. Doing business in Japan goes way beyond finding a shrewd attorney to hammer out a deal and then going through the motions of the project on autopilot.

Finally, contracts serve as control instruments between unequal partners. For your situation, this should matter less, since I hope you bring something to the table that your Japanese business partners want and need. They should see you as an equal. However, there exist many unequal business relationships in Asia. When a small company depends on a bigger one, for example to distribute a product, it would chain itself to the bigger company to get access to distribution channels. Such arrangements are often extremely unbalanced, where small companies give up rights that those in the West never would. I mention this type of deal for the sake of completeness. You should always try to enter into equal partnerships with Japanese business partners from the beginning.

Now you know that there is no need to hammer out every last detail of legal agreements in Japan. However, the three important parts where you should be firm are how you define damages, anything related to payments, and what is excluded from the contract. We will discuss them later in this chapter.

Business Lesson

Contracts have different functions that depend on the corporate culture of your counterparties. Find out how they understand contracts to save yourself additional expenses and grief once your projects are underway.

Specify Damages

Like we just learned, it is a good idea to avoid too much depth in your contracts with Japanese partners. Much of it is up for interpretation anyway, so you may just be wasting time by drilling down into every eventuality in negotiations. However, one of the areas you should be clear about is what attorneys call "liquidated damages." This term describes the penalty for counterparties when they breach the deal. To address this issue correctly, your contract needs to define at least two things:

- How you define a breach of contract and
- the amount of money that your counterparty has to pay in case of a breach.

Breach of contract can take many forms. It can happen through negligence of others, a sudden low priority of your project, delays that were easy to prevent or willful disregard of terms of the deal. Let's say you negotiated a compensation schedule where you receive 1/3 of your fee upon signing the contract, 1/3 halfway into the deal, and 1/3 upon delivery of the final project. A common issue with Japanese companies is that they pay the first installment promptly, but later suggests to pay you the remaining 2/3 of the fee upon delivery. If you trust the other party and are comfortable with this, then go for it. You will have a return favor that you can cash in later. But if prefer the original payment schedule, you need to exert pressure. Stiff penalties in case of late payments help you to do this. Unless you clearly specify them, you will be on shaky ground to enforce a contract in a Japanese court.

Another example of a breach is a project that never completes without your fault. It is possible that your Japanese counterparty loses interest in the project or never planned to see it through in the first place. They may never tell you their true intentions but will degrade the project to the point where it has either no resources or milestones are postponed continually. In this case, you need to have a clear definition of what needs to happen. Renegotiating deals later is how Japanese address most of these issues. It is OK to play along with it if this is to your advantage, too. But if it unilaterally serves their interests, you need to put your foot down. If you have clearly specified damages in your deal, you can point out they need to pay a penalty unless they honor their promise. Since losing face is a big deal in Japan, you use their corporate culture to your advantage here. In any event, if you forget to specify damages, you give up much of your power, which can cost you dearly.

Business Lesson

Address breach of contract and damages payable in your contracts. Only if you have spelled out these terms clearly in black and white, will you be able to put your foot down when it matters.

When It Comes to Money, Be a Stickler

It goes without saying that you need to be clear about compensation in your business deals. Who pays for what needs to be laid out precisely. As always, better avoid relying on oral promises. When it comes to money, the fun stops. Promises that involve compensation need to be in writing.

For example, let's look at travel expenses. If you do business abroad, things can get expensive very fast. If you provide a service but your main place of business is outside of Japan, you need to fly back and forth, rent hotel rooms and cars to get around. Better have a clear idea of this cost before you start a project. If there is any ambiguity in a contract about who foots the bill for travel expenses, then you need to go back to your attorney and hammer out this point.

Another thing you need to be clear about is the payment schedule. When will you receive payment? If you agree on a schedule of 1/3, 1/3, 1/3, what is the definition of "half-way through the project" and "upon delivery?" Better add dates or a number of days after signing the contract for payment milestones. Ask your attorney how to do this best.

There is a saying that contracts are unnecessary until things turn sour. This is true, of course. We humans avoid imagining the worst and prefer hoping that everything will be roses. However, when things become difficult and you or your business partners want out of a deal, it helps if at least the points about payment are clear. If you omitted to pay attention here, you are in a weak position, especially when you are on your foreign business partners' turf. Avoid this by eliminating ambiguity about money, including the amount payable and when payments need to occur.

Business Lesson

Avoid ambiguity about money, expenses and payment schedules in your contracts. Especially when things turn sour, you need to have clarity at least in this point.

Ask for as Much as Possible Upfront

When you work as a service provider, it is common to include a payment schedule in your contracts. Normally this would be something along the lines of 1/3, 1/3, 1/3, as we already discussed earlier. However, payment schedules vary widely. For example, some service providers and consultants work on a results basis, where they receive the entire payment only when the project has concluded successfully.

When you do business in Japan, I recommend you ask for as much as possible upfront. Why? First of all, let's assume the project stalls midway, which is quite common in Japan. Would you rather have nothing or fifty percent of your fee at this point? When your project was expensive, someone will have a lot of explaining to do when they stop it midway or admit it was a mistake in the first place. The more your Japanese business partner has invested in you, the higher their incentive to see the project through. Whenever possible, they will avoid losing face, which can be to your advantage only if they already went out on a limb and paid you a high advance. If your advance was a thousand dollars, they may cancel your project without much pain. But if it was a million...

I know we all want to avoid coming across as greedy. Despite the fact that we love Japan, its people and its culture, we need to be aware of the real the possibility of losing money when we do business there. Even if you managed to command a high advance for your project, you may never see the rest of the money. When your business partners balk at the high upfront cost, you can always offer to pay them back everything if the quality of your work is not satisfactory. Ask your attorney how to formulate this properly.

Whenever you are at the mercy of foreign business partners and things turn out to be less rosy than expected, you will be at a disadvantage. Avoid this by asking for a high advance payment. This will also inform you of the determination of your business partners to work with you under fair conditions.

Business lesson

Command high fees for your work and ask for as much as possible in advance. This gives you a better chance to complete your project because your counterparty has a bigger loss if they stall or cancel it. Offer to pay back the advance if the quality of your work is unsatisfactory.

Limit Your Deals

Now you know that you should pay attention to details related to fees and damages in your contracts with Japanese counterparties. The third important part in contracts is what is excluded from the deal. For example, items you could exclude from your deals are:

- Intellectual property rights;
- Copyrights and other usage rights;
- Travel expenses beyond a certain number of trips;
- Changes in deliverables beyond a certain number;
- Reports and documentation;
- Meetings beyond a certain number;
- Non-compete clauses.

The first two items mattered in my project. Many different rights for usage and distribution exist in the music business, and I paid less attention than I should have to defining them clearly in the deal. As we already learned earlier, when it came to the publishing rights, the Japanese record label assumed that they would be available at no cost. Since the deal said nothing about these particular rights, they claimed it was only natural that they were included. In reality, this is the most valuable part of a music project. Artists signed with a major label can sell these rights expensively and they are a major part of their income. Because my deal was unclear in this point, unnecessary arguments began that led to the demise of the entire project. You can avoid them easily if you include a few sentences addressing the issues you think may lead to discussions later on.

Western contracts address most of the potential grey areas. In Japanese contracts, however, they are left opaque on purpose. Later, when the project has started, you will learn that your counterparty assumed they would be included in the deal. The one who is losing here is you, especially when you find yourself doing business abroad. Clearly define what is excluded. Think about all the extras that projects in your field normally entail. When you get the feeling your counterparty might have a different opinion about certain points, then describe them in the deal. As always, look at the contract from their perspective and imagine which issues could be problem areas.

When you specify what is excluded in your projects, you give the other party less opportunities to start arguments and stall your projects. When they do that, it is up to you to push back. Just as important as saying what you want is what you exclude from a contract. When you do this, you are on much steadier ground.

Business Lesson

Clearly state in your contracts what is excluded, for example travel expenses or intellectual property. Even though you might assume certain points are obvious, still briefly address them. This can save you much trouble and arguments later.

Avoid Indentured Servitude

The Japanese are big believers in protectionism, the practice of shielding a country's domestic industries from foreign competition with high taxes on imports. This policy is often one-sided. It helps keep the competition out, but enables a country to spread their products around the world at competitive prices. The Japanese themselves certainly believe their economic success has been a result of protectionism. No one of any standing in business, government or academia believes that Japan's success has been a result of free trade.[14]

Protectionist thinking finds its way into contract negotiations as well, regardless of how small the projects are. When you understand where the Japanese are coming from, it will be easier to spot one-sided deal terms that are perfectly common for them, but a great disadvantage for you. Such

---

[14] Fletcher, Ian. Japan, the Forgotten Protectionist Threat. Huffington Post, April 17, 2011. http://www.huffingtonpost.com/ian-fletcher/japan-the-forgotten-prote_b_850269.html.

terms could be:

- A promise to provide your services exclusively to one company for X years at a very low price;
- A distribution agreement lasting for perpetuity, with no option for you to cancel;
- High damages when you want to exit the contract, but complete freedom for the other party;
- High commissions on your sales payable to a gatekeeper.

Especially when you are starting out in business, such deal terms are common. This can happen anywhere and is by no means exclusive to Japan. However, I have seen many Japanese entrepreneurs sign such deals. Whenever they dealt with companies bigger than theirs, they actually expected one-sided terms. They were unaware that the contracts were inherently unfair and nothing short of indentured servitude. Nobody ever told them there was another way to work together, for example the idea of win-win.

Indentured servitude is quite common in Asia. When you spot blatantly one-sided deal terms, try to push back. When that is impossible, find other business partners. If they see you as inferior, you will have a hard time to establish the kind of business relationship that will help you prosper. Better find people who see you as a talented equal and like to do business with you. They exist everywhere.

Business Lesson

When deal terms are blatantly one-sided to your disadvantage, immediately push back. If the other party refuses to give in, part ways. Life is too short for indentured servitude.

Beware of Empty Promises

Let's get deeper into the context of negotiating deals. For the Japanese, the signature in the contract is a signal that both parties are willing to move ahead in a hopefully mutually beneficial professional relationship. We already know that the contents of the deal are less important and subject to change in the course of the project. It should therefore hardly surprise us that Japanese business partners will want to push things towards a signature as quickly as possible.

To move negotiations forward, they will try to establish goodwill. They hope to speed things along by inviting you to lavish meals and cultural events such as sumo wrestling or arts festivals. In their mind, this establishes a debt on your part that should mollify you to move forward in good faith. If it takes a few promises about other deals that may spring out of this project, this is also just a means to an end. If you keep hammering away in the fine print of the deal at this point, you misunderstand what your partners are trying to do. Better let certain points in the project open. Most importantly, avoid writing in new promises that are largely rhetorical. They may never materialize and are just a sign of their goodwill if you also accommodate them. You should take whatever is said and done to wrap up negotiations with a handful of salt. When you are aware of this dynamic, the negotiation process and the project itself will go smoother and make much more sense.

Business Lesson

Some business partners try to accelerate negotiations with gifts and promises about future projects. This is often an attempt to establish goodwill in their favor with little intention to follow through. Be aware of this dynamic to save yourself disappointment later down the road.

Over-promise

Just as your Japanese business partners promise you the moon, feel free to make informal promises yourself in the negotiation phase of the deal. This may seem underhanded to you, but it is common practice in Japan. Of course, make sure that none of the promises find their way into the written contract.

When you want to establish a good business climate, you could promise the following to your counterparty:

- They will get exposure abroad by working with you;
- You will recommend clients to them if the project goes well;
- You will work on the next project at a discount.

If your counterparty asks you for deliverables that are beyond the scope of the current agreement, the answer is always "yes." Depending on how things go you can still adjust your promises later down the road. This is how the Japanese do it and you can do the same.

Business Lesson

Promise your counterparty additional benefits that are outside the scope of the deal. These can be exposure, recommendations, or future discounts. They get the other party more invested in the project and can help you speed up negotiations.

Look Out for Yourself

Despite their philosophy of seeking harmony in personal and professional relationships, nobody expects you to become Japanese just because you have a project in Japan. Your business ventures are most likely motivated by more than establishing harmony and good karma. You need to understand where the Japanese are coming from, which is the reason why we discussed some of the philosophies that guide their decisions in business and in life. Knowing how they think will make it easier for you to set up networks, meetings and business deals. Nevertheless, even though a project takes place in Japan, your own opinion matters just as much as theirs.

Regardless of the fact that their philosophies are attractive, expect from the Japanese that they also understand your position and cultural background. At the end of the day, this is a partnership and not a one-sided relationship where one party dictates how the other party should think and act. Keep your identity and your personal goals intact. Demand from your counterparty what you want. Otherwise, they will rarely give it to you. You will have to make some concessions, but still see to it that the deal terms measure up to your expectations and professional standards.

By now you have learned how the Japanese frame discussions and how they express their agreement or disagreement. Employ the same techniques to persistently push them towards where you want the deal to go. Unless you do this, you will find yourself in a corner before you know it, with the option to either accept the terms or walk. The exotic and strange customs of Japan have a seductive power over foreigners and can make them feel insecure. Play along to a degree, but keep looking out for yourself.

Business Lesson

Despite the culture and customs of your host, make sure a business deal is right for you in the first place. Play along with some of the customs and rituals they may have, but keep an eye on your personal goals at all times.

Negotiate in English if Possible

When you do business in a foreign country, there will always be a language barrier. If you are from America or Europe and you engage in a business deal with a Japanese counterparty, the language in the project will most likely be English. While basic Japanese conversation is logical and relatively straightforward to pick up, formal Japanese is extremely complicated. It would be unreasonable of your business partner to expect from you and your attorney to understand a Japanese contract. That leaves you with two options: Get an attorney in Japan or negotiate in English.

Better refrain from offering to hire a Japanese attorney. A law firm that is fluent in both Japanese and English will be very expensive. Most Japanese companies with overseas operations are used to the language issue and retain attorneys in England and America. Try to push your deal through this channel. If you bring in your own English-speaking attorney, you will be at an advantage.

When you negotiate face to face in Japan, your Japanese business partner will most likely have someone available who can translate. Members of their management team may have studied abroad and may be fairly fluent in English. Most of the time, there is no need for you to hire a translator yourself. When writing the contract, the best situation for you is to hire the legal team you use for all your other deals as well. Unless your law firm already has experience in dealing with Japanese clients, then you should involve yourself in drafting the deal. With the help of these business lessons, you will be able to advise your lawyer how to find a compromise and avoid a stalemate in negotiations.

Business Lesson

Negotiate contracts in English and avoid foreign law firms or translating contracts. Foreign multinational organizations have legal professionals in English-speaking jurisdictions. Use this channel for your projects abroad.

Keep Things Simple

When your legal team is working on a contract with your business partners in Japan, make things easy to understand for the Japanese. They will also have an English-speaking law firm, of course. Nevertheless, they will still have to translate the entire contract so the executives in Japan will understand what is going on. This is a considerable expense and you should be happy that you managed to offload it to your counterparty.

In exchange, try to make things easy for them to understand by avoiding excessive use of boilerplate. This is the standardized, uniform language often found in legal documents, such as "not withstanding the foregoing." Even though these terms make it easier for your lawyer to draft and read a contract, they are difficult to translate in a foreign language. Convince your attorney to go light on boilerplate and outline the agreement in plain English. This speeds up responses from your Japanese counterparty, and it looks like you have nothing to hide.

I avoid boilerplate in all my contracts, not just in those with foreign clients. The better the people you do business with can understand contracts without help from their lawyers, the stronger are the business relationships that you will build.

Business Lesson

Avoid boilerplate in legal agreements whenever possible. This may speed up negotiations if your counterparty has to translate the contract, and it looks more transparent. Your business partners will actually understand the contract without help from their attorney.

Deliver Upon Payment

I had compiled all necessary files for my Japanese music project on several DVDs. Because the record company was eager to wrap up a milestone, they needed these files. I met with them in their conference room in Tokyo to discuss how things would progress from here on. They had grand plans, and a newly hired MBA from Todai University explained them to me in vague terms and heavily accented English. Then he asked for the DVDs. Like a stack of chips in the casino, I placed them in the middle of the table. The MBA pulled them towards him with both hands. He looked like someone who had just won the jackpot. Then we parted ways. This would be the last time I set foot in the offices of that record company. A week later I received an email mentioning that the money had run out to see this project through. You already know the rest of this story.

The lesson here is that you should never deliver anything without first being paid. If a lot of money is at stake and your foreign business partners have already decided to terminate the project, what incentive do they have to pay you? If they concluded in their mind that this was the first and last project they did with you, you will never see a dime. Yes, you can always sue them in court, but I would advise you to do anything you can to avoid that. When you deliver the goods, suggest a one-for-one exchange. They can pay you in cash, of wire the funds to you before you deliver. This is the Wild-West way of doing business, and it still works.

Of course, you need to sugarcoat this a little bit. Even if you mistrust your counterparty, you should never bring that across. You could offer a discount of ten percent if they pay you in cash. Mention that this is what your business partner back home demanded you to do, since it is common practice with your firm. Be friendly and politely insist. If they refuse, you also withdraw and stall with your delivery. This may remind you of high school. But when it is about getting paid or not, it is all the while worth the trouble. Unless you are smart about your finances, business partners will rarely take you seriously.

Business Lesson

With new business partners, make it a rule to deliver upon payment only. Especially if they are abroad, you will have no recourse if they decide not to pay.

CHAPTER 6: HOW TO MANAGE PEOPLE AND PROJECTS

You have landed a deal, and it is time to get started with the project. Now the real work begins. Managing your clients and your own team is exciting and a challenge at the same time. Especially when you work internationally, you need to arm yourself with diverse strategies to motivate all the people involved. This chapter explains some of the Japanese strategies to do that.

Smells Like Team Spirit

More than anything else, the Japanese value to work in teams. Completing a task as efficiently as possible is less important than the whole team accomplishing a worthwhile goal together. Meetings and discussions take place to make sure everybody is on the same page so the project goes as planned. This leads to a different perception of time during business hours. Nothing should be rushed or pushed through. "Thinking outside the box" to find a shortcut is rare, even unpopular. The Japanese approach always ends with a result that is unanimously acceptable. Individuals will stay in the office long after they have checked off the tasks assigned to them. Unless the entire team has achieved their common goal, they are available for help and support.

Because they function as a group, most Japanese workers see it as their responsibility to stay with others while they are still working. Late hours are the result of a sense of solidarity and have little to do with an enormous workload or perfectionism. This prevents them from using their full vacation time. For this reason, Japanese companies shut down completely for one week in spring and summer so employees get some guilt-fee time with their families. The same reasoning applies to company trips, where the whole unit goes away for a few days together on the company's dime.

This Japanese work ethic seemed terribly ineffective to me when I first encountered it. Indeed, it is a mystery to many foreigners. If they are in charge, they often assign new tasks to those seemingly idle workers. However, this conflicts with the sense of team work and destroys the balance in the office. You must understand how the Japanese like to work if you are in a leadership position. At the same time, make sure the team as a whole has a clearly defined goal. Better benchmark the deliverables of teams and not those of individuals.

Business Lesson

Some cultures value team work over individual achievements. If this is the case in your project, give clear deliverables to the team and break them down into tasks for each team member. Instead of loading new work on those who have accomplished their tasks, better ask them to help others finish theirs.

Self-starters Are Rare

As one would expect of a people who appreciate group think, personal expression and individuality are rare in Japan. Executives are notorious for risk-aversion and slow decision making. This attitude trickles down through all ranks. In a traditional Japanese company, people will do what they are told. Unless they have clear instructions, they will rarely go out on a limb. Self-starters in the Western sense are therefore extremely hard to find.

But what about the new generation of young Japanese entrepreneurs who have studied abroad? As ambassadors of Western entrepreneurship, they profess they are ready to reinvent the way things are done in the homeland. This is a commendable goal, however, when you look underneath the surface, it becomes clear that all they apply is a watered-down, Japanese version of Western entrepreneurship. In a country where ninety-nine percent of the workforce shies away from taking initiative, how successful can they be? Without noticing it, they tone down their vision until their practices resemble those of the local companies. This may sound unfair, but have you heard of a groundbreaking startup from Japan recently? When you understand how the Japanese did business through the ages and are still doing it, this hardly comes as a surprise.

When you are a self-starter yourself, it is easy to expect that you will find like-minded people abroad. My own search was far less successful than I hoped. I love my Japanese friends, but taking bold risks and initiative are not their strengths. When you need self-starters for a project in the Far East, better hire foreigners. If you depend on innovative human capital abroad, either bring it with you or source it from a group with a good track record. The habit of taking initiative is hard to teach, and trying to do that will cost you time and money, without achieving the results you desire.

Business Lesson

If the success of a project abroad depends on innovative human capital, best bring it with you. If you source it locally, tap into groups with a strong track record of achievement. Unless people already possess them, these skills are hard to teach.

Be Dedicated and Thoughtful

Crafting a samurai sword (刀, *katana*) is a lengthy and complex endeavor. The sword smith begins by repeatedly folding and welding pieces of high and low carbon steel to work out the impurities in the metal. This special steel can contain thousands of individual layers. The smith attains the curvature of a katana by a process of differential hardening. He coats the blade with layers of wet clay, the edge with a thinner layer than the sides and spine of the sword. Then he heats it and quenches it in water or oil. The slurry causes only the edge of the blade to be hardened, which causes the blade to curve due to the difference in densities of the micro-structures in the steel. This process creates a distinct line down the sides of the blade called the *hamon* (刃文, blade pattern). Each pattern and each smith's style of pattern is distinct. Finally, after forging the blade, the smith polishes it between one and three weeks. He uses finer and finer grains of polishing stones in the process until the blade has a mirror finish. However, the blunt edge of the katana often receives a matte finish to emphasize the blade pattern. All things considered, making a high-quality katana usually takes several months.

Why is this important to know? It isn't. But it shows how much weight the Japanese put on paying attention to what one does. I experienced this first-hand when I had been invited to a Japanese sushi restaurant, apparently the best in Japan, called *Sukiyabashi Jiro*. The dinner was very expensive and very delicious, but I found even more interesting what was going on behind the scenes. Several apprentices prepared the fish, the rice and the seaweed, and all the main sushi chef had to do was put together the pieces in front of the customer. I later became aware that these apprentices learn how to roast seaweed for several years. Then they graduate to cooking rice. And then, maybe, they get to cut and prepare the fish. To become a full-fledged sushi chef in this restaurant takes about ten years of apprenticeship. I found this incredible. In the West, where everybody thinks he is a natural genius who can wing it when he really has to, such dedication is rare.

The art of thoughtful practice is what matters to people in Japan. You notice this everywhere around you. Nowhere else in the world have I seen builders lay tile with such concentration, cut wood with the sharpest edges, or prepare the perfect cup of green tea in a process that included a hundred individual steps. Nonetheless, nobody expects the same level of dedication from you. But what they expect is that you take your work seriously, give it your full attention and put forth your best effort. Even if all you do is go through the motions, at least look like there is no job more important in the world. This will make an impression in Japan and abroad.

Business Lesson

When you work, concentrate fully on what you do. Even if it is a rote process, focus your undivided attention on it. This helps you avoid distractions, work faster, and create output of higher quality.

Brace for Inefficiency but Expect Results

Because of their sense of solidarity with the team, most Japanese work more than their Western counterparts. Even though the official business hours may be 9 AM to 6 PM, most Japanese are in the office one hour earlier and stay until several hours later. Employees are rarely reporting overtime, and most of these extra hours never show up in the statistics.

Even though employees may be doing a terrific job as individuals, unless they blend in with the team, they will acquire the reputation of being selfish and unfit for teamwork. Staying in the office for an extra two hours, mostly rearranging papers on the desk or playing computer games, seems inefficient to any foreigner. For a Japanese worker, however, this time is well spent and necessary. In case of an emergency or unexpected need of a colleague, he or she is promptly available to help. To be fair, overtime is often a far cry from busy work. The Japanese are just present during this time. The only catch is that they should look alert and ready for action. Reading a book or chatting with coworkers is taboo. Playing a computer game or writing one's blog is fine. Doing anything that closely resembles work is acceptable. Such a work environment is sharply at odds with the Western way of doing things.

Like everyone else, I had some difficulty understanding this mindset. Teamwork often seemed a pretext to me to cover up the laziness of some of the staff. But one thing surprised me: The Japanese teams always delivered. If individuals are in charge, their performance is often hit or miss. In the Japanese system, the end result is always at least average, never a complete disaster. They often took longer than what I thought was necessary. However, the entire team felt developed a sense of accomplishment and belonging each time they completed a project. This made it worth putting up with some of the inefficiency.

I tried to set up a teamwork mindset in my other projects in Southeast Asia and in Europe. Most of these efforts failed. Unless solidarity is deeply ingrained in the corporate culture of a country, people will rarely pull together as a team. If you have to explain to them what teamwork is, you are already losing ground. Better understand the preferred work modality of people and then adjust to it.

Business Lesson

Understand how people like to work, as individuals or as teams. Adapt to their style, even if it seems inefficient. Trying to introduce a new culture often fails. Unless it emerged organically over time, you can rarely expect good results.

Blend In Outwardly

When you work with Japanese staff, you will have to change your ways somewhat to accommodate them, otherwise, they will felt lost at sea. They may pretend to understand what you mean when you say you need them to work "independently." When you suggest they become "self-starters," they may nod their head in agreement. Regardless, you will find the results of such efforts wanting. If you work with a Japanese team or are part of one yourself, you need to adjust to their culture. There is no way around it.

However, as so many things in Japan, you only need to adhere to the *letter* of the law. Secretly, you can still bend its spirit however you want. When the rules demand you stay in the office until a project is finished, happily comply. But instead of wasting time waiting around, work on your own projects. Prepare other tasks that may come due much later in the pipeline. Whenever you work, be visible. Whenever you are visible, make it look like you are working hard. Sooner or later you will have cleared your entire pipeline for months to come. This will give you a lot of free time to network within the company, suggest improvements for other projects, or start new ones altogether.

If you lead a team and find their output substandard, start allocating tasks in a different way. Stay within the parameters of the framework, but adjust whatever you see fit. An outsider's perspective sometimes brings improvements. When your ideas function within the age-old template, they will get much better results.

Business Lesson

If your project spans different cultures and work ethics, do your work in the same way like a local person or company – at least outwardly. For yourself, work smarter. Avoid wasting time or being visible without producing anything. Instead, finish your entire pipeline of tasks to free up time for new projects.

Plan for Contingencies – the Japanese Way

Regardless of your meticulous planning, things may turn out differently from what you expected them to be. When this happens in your native environment, you know where to go. You may have a support team that can help you out, and your clients will understand when force majeure took the project off its planned trajectory. You can manage unforeseen events and avert a catastrophe because you are walking on familiar ground.

Unfortunately, this is not the case in Japan. Even the simplest issues can end up costing you a lot of time. Assume a business partner hired a car for you to drive you to a meeting somewhere on the outskirts of Tokyo. You already waited outside your hotel for half an hour and there is still no car in sight. Calls to the business partner's phone go to his Japanese voicemail. There seem to be no taxis in the neighborhood. Oh, wait, here is one. You tell the taxi driver the name and the place of the company, but all he does is shake his head. All I could do in situations like these was wait for the business partner to return the call, who apologized and postponed the meeting to the next day. My trip was already packed and I had to skip the meeting, even though it was one of the main reasons I had come to Tokyo.

Notice a pattern here? I *assumed* that things would work out as planned but did not verify or have a backup plan ready. We already learned that the Japanese are often too shy to say "no." The potential for misunderstandings is huge. People may fail to deliver what they promised. If they do, fall back on plan B. You need to plan for contingencies in Japan.

How do the Japanese handle this? Here is a simple trick. Make the person who is responsible for something a vital part of it. If someone organized a meeting for you, ask him or her to join you. Offer to pick up the person at a place you know and then go there together. Likewise, when someone is supposed to deliver something critical, help them do it. Instead of hoping they follow through on their own, be there when they do. Use the philosophy of team work to your advantage to accomplish your goals.

Business Lesson

Plan for contingencies by involving other people in your plans. If they made a promise to deliver a critical asset, help them do it. Instead of assuming that things work out, give others a vested interest in a positive outcome.

Take Care of Critical Tasks Yourself

Even though you can make others part of your projects in ways we just learned, things can still turn sour. Especially when this is your first project in Japan, everything needs to go smoothly to lay the foundation for follow-up business. When it comes to deadlines, critical milestones, business presentations and other critical collateral in your project, go the extra mile and see them through yourself.

Does this mean you need to assume the worst from everybody on your Japanese team? Yes and no. Let them do the work they are capable to do. However, be aware that you as the project lead are ultimately responsible for delivery. If you fail to plan accordingly, the blame will land in your court. How did I handle this when I was working in Japan? I scheduled critical deadlines several days earlier than necessary. I also made sure that I had enough time to troubleshoot any potential issues that could hamper successful delivery. This often entailed trivial tasks like quality control of data or making bound prints in a copy shop for a presentation.

It is often these simple things that will put a project on the rocks. The big issues always seem to sort themselves out in one way or another. Unless you take responsibility for critical tasks yourself, you may be gambling on the future of your project.

Business Lesson

Assign tasks to capable members of your team, but take responsibility for the critical deliverables yourself. These are often the seemingly minor issues in a project. Identify them beforehand and allocate enough time to make sure they are perfect.

Keep Your Emotions to Yourself

The Japanese frown upon anyone and anything that disturbs their beloved harmony. Even in the most upsetting of circumstances have I seen them keep composed to preserve it. Stoically, they suffered what was inevitable, swallowed their pride and then acted as if nothing had happened. What they did or thought in private is another story. As long as none of it is visible on the outside, they are fine. When you work in such an environment, people expect the same behavior from you. Even though your culture and upbringing may encourage you to let your feelings out instead of bottling them up, angry outbursts will cause trouble for you in Japan. I already mentioned my unwarranted use of one single F-bomb earlier in this book. It took several hours to smooth over its effect. You need to use your time for more productive things.

Japan taught me that I needed to pause and reflect before taking action. This was difficult for a European who had lived in Los Angeles a quarter of his life. I grew up with the beliefs that spontaneity wins the day, that we were thinking too much and that rules were made to be broken. All this advice proved impractical in Japan. Biting my lip proved to be an important skill I picked up over the years.

The Japanese know how different people from the West think about expressing their discontent. In isolated instances they may test their resolve to adjust to the Japanese ways. They may try to provoke you, just to see if you can keep your cool. This can also happen under the pretext of "being drunk" on a night out. When that happens, you already know what to do. Recognize the attempts for what they are and take the high road. Play along and keep your opinion to yourself.

Just as you should keep negative emotions to yourself, the same applies to positive emotions as well. Let's assume you just found out you won the lottery while you are out with Japanese business partners. Do you jump up and down and tell everyone of your windfall? Maybe in the West, but not in

Japan. Being more fortunate than others also disturbs the equilibrium. Some people may feel jealous and will harbor ill feelings toward you, and there goes the harmony. Happy emotions can land you in hot water just as much as an angry outburst. Outwardly always blend into the mainstream by coming across as balanced and a little boring. In private you are free to do whatever you like.

Business Lesson

Some cultures frown upon public display of emotions, both negative and positive. Anything that departs from the average may challenge the equilibrium of situations. Better keep your feelings to yourself in business. In private you can do whatever you like.

Appear Like a Humble Genius

Japanese people admire big feats of memory, intelligence, business savvy and sportsmanship. Even though you should avoid bragging about your accomplishments, you should use them to your advantage. The best possible image in Japan is the one of the humble genius, superstar, or millionaire. You may think that you are humble, but if you are like me, you will consider yourself anything but a genius. At the same time, think about this: What compels you to believe that you of all people can pull off a project, in Japan or anywhere else? The number of successful entrepreneurs is very small. Those who have the nerve to go out on a limb and declare they are going to make it must have something special. This alone sets the stage for your entrance as a business genius. If you hang up your shingle in Japan and make it known that you plan to be a successful entrepreneur, they will automatically believe you possess extraordinary skills. This is already half the rent.

In other words, the Japanese will overestimate you for a while. What you should do in such a situation is take advantage of it. Whenever you can, make things look effortless to you. If you need to stay up all night to finish a project, make an effort to look as fresh as a daisy the next morning. When you just pulled something off that nobody believed you could, keep it to yourself that you were surprised yourself. Take the credit without making a fuss and then humbly continue your work.

Outperform in the first weeks and months of a project. Work more, harder and better than anybody else. Before you know it, you will have acquired the image of nothing short but a genius. Once established, this reputation will go a long way. Those around you will broadcast it to their networks on your behalf, which will downplay your success even more. When that happens, chances are you can benefit from this reputation for a long time. Launching and running projects abroad is already hard enough. Get all the help you can to make it work.

Business Lesson

When a project begins, work harder and smarter than anybody else. Your superior results should look effortless. When others share the tales of the miracles you achieved, you acquire the reputation of a humble genius.

Deliver at the Last Minute

We already learned that in Japan, more important than completing a task as quickly as possible is the consensus of the group. This thinking rarely speed up projects. In fact, teamwork is often slower than a sprint by a dedicated individual. Even when you work as a team of one or with your own staff, you should do the same with your projects. In front of your Japanese business partners, make your work look like teamwork, even if it is anything but.

Now how do you do that? One strategy is deliver your projects right at the deadline. If your project has a generous schedule, you will rarely impress your Japanese partners by delivering early. Much better is to use the extra time to enhance the quality of your work. In Japan, the best possible product matters, not the fastest possible. By delivering as late as possible, you show that you understand that.

Does this mean that you have to toil tirelessly until the last minute, even though your team completed the project in half the allocated time? Of course not. Just work leisurely once you have ticked all the necessary boxes of your deliverables. Then deliver at the due date and point out all the extras you included. There is another reason to avoid finishing early in Japan, and once more, it has to do with *wa* (harmony). Delivering at the deadline shows that the person who set it knows their job and estimated the right amount of time necessary to produce high-quality work. You indirectly make them look more competent.

Business Lesson

Some business cultures value higher quality more than quick completion of a project. If you have extra time, use it to make the project better, but never deliver early.

CHAPTER 7: PRODUCTIVITY HACKS

Work fills up most of the waking hours of the average adult. Because they work longer hours, the work-life balance of the Japanese is even more tipped towards their jobs. To keep up with stress and increase their alertness, they use several unique hacks that help them stay focused. This chapter introduces a few of the unconventional techniques I encountered in Japan. Please use them with care and evaluate yourself if they make sense for you. They are just some ideas to show you how the Japanese hack their creative energy.

Snacks and Green Tea

Even though most Japanese are relatively slim, they are snackoholics. Go to the snacks isle of any Japanese supermarket and revel in the overwhelming sea of *Pocky*, *Koala's March*, *Mushroom Mountain* and all the other sweet and savory treats.[15] They provide the perfect fuel when you need an extra boost in the mid morning or afternoon. Most people I worked with in Tokyo were big fans of these snacks. They ate relatively little during lunch, but stocked up on treats from *7Eleven* or *Family Mart* to get through the afternoon. Eating several small meals and snacks during the day can increase your energy. Experiment if it works for you.

After drinking water, tea is the most consumed beverage in the world. Most people are familiar with fermented teas, such as black tea. Green tea is a non-fermented tea of the same leaves. It contains more antioxidants, minerals and vitamins than black tea. Since ancient times, green tea is considered a healthy beverage in traditional medicine. Among numerous health benefits, recent studies suggest that it may contribute to a reduction in the risk of cardiovascular disease.[16] Even though green tea contains slightly less caffeine than black tea, I find it more stimulating than black tea or coffee.[17] Perhaps it is a compound effect of its other ingredients, but it definitely makes me more alert and less jittery. Try for yourself if green tea is a healthy energy booster for you as well.

---

[15] Wikipedia. List of Japanese Sweets.
http://en.wikipedia.org/wiki/List_of_Japanese_snacks.
[16] Journal of the American College of Nutrition. Beneficial Effects of Green Tea - A Review. Volume 25, Issue 2, 2006.
http://www.tandfonline.com/doi/abs/10.1080/07315724.2006.10719518.
[17] Caffeine Informer. Green Tea Caffeine Levels.
http://www.caffeineinformer.com/caffeine-content/green-tea.

Business Lesson

Eat smaller meals and supplement them with snacks throughout the day to keep your energy levels constant. Try a loose-leaf green tea instead of coffee. It has healthy ingredients beyond caffeine.

Cat Naps

I was surprised when my Japanese business partners told me about their sleeping schedules. They would usually go to bed very late, between one and two in the morning. Most of them were up again around six. This gave them somewhere between four and five hours of sleep. Just the thought of it made me want to lie down and take a nap. Then I discovered that was exactly what most of them did. They would sleep on the train to the office. If they drove somewhere during the day in a cab, they would close their eyes and use the fifteen minutes in the car to get some rest. During the lunch break it was quite common to see them leaned against a wall "meditating." Others would rest their head on the table in front of them until a buzzer on their phone went off.

Did you know it is perfectly acceptable to sleep in the office in Japan? Of course, this comes with a catch: You should look like you could jolt up at any second and resume your work. Resting your head on your desk is fine. But slouching comfortably in your chair is off limits. It also helps if you look extremely exhausted. Being lazy is no reason to take a cat nap, but staving off a collapse is.

Taking short naps during the day can help you cut down on your sleep time. A good night's rest is still much better than just a few hours of sleep at night with several cat naps during the day. But when I had little sleep and feel my energy draining away, closing my eyes for a few minutes often helps restore it.

Business Lesson

When you feel tired during the day, close your eyes for a few minutes and take a cat nap. This is often more effective than dosing with vitamins or caffeine.

Aromatherapy

Perhaps you are familiar with the Japanese chain store *Muji*. It sells household and consumer goods distinguished by minimalism in design, emphasis on recycling and a no-logo policy.[18] The stores have branched out in the last years beyond Japan into every bigger city in the world. When you stroll through a Muji shop, you will have noticed several types of vaporizers and diffusers for essential oils. They always seemed like novelty items to me until I moved to Tokyo. Many offices and households have aroma diffusers in constant use.

Using aromas to create a positive mood has been popular in Japan for a long time. About 1,400 years ago, the Japanese developed a traditional system of incense and aromatherapy called *kodo*. It consisted of burning fragrant woods, flowers and spices. The Japanese describe the process of experiencing the fragrance as "listening to the incense," not smelling it.[19] Kodo is considered an art form similar to calligraphy or arranging flowers (ikebana). Scenting their bodies, clothes, homes and shops is a natural practice to improve harmony and health. The Japanese welcome anything that upgrades their immediate surroundings.

Using scents as a stimulant is still in demand in Japan. Many office workers have an aroma diffuser on their desks or carry small bottles of essential oils with them from which they take a whiff now and then. These oils are available in supermarkets and organic food shops. Pick one that you like and carry a small bottle with you. Aromas can help you charge your batteries naturally when you need a boost.

Business Lesson

Use natural oils to wake up or for a boost of energy. Citrus and mint fragrances work well. You can use them in an aroma diffuser or put a small drop on a handkerchief on your desk.

---

[18] Wikipedia. Muji. http://en.wikipedia.org/wiki/Muji.
[19] The Kyoto Project. Japanese Aromatherapy: Kodo. http://thekyotoproject.org/english/japanese-aromatherapy-kodo/.

Look at a Cute Animal

Pretty mascots like *Hello Kitty* or *Alpacasso*, anime characters with their big eyes, and countless little charms for cell phones have done their best to promote *kawaii*, the Japanese word for "cute," to the world. Cute things are popular because they produce positive feelings. Research suggests that there may be more to this than meets the eye. A study at Hiroshima University found that looking at cute images promotes a more careful behavior and narrows focus. When university students performed a fine motor dexterity task after viewing images of baby animals, their performance increased by an average of forty-three percent. Performance in visual search tasks improved by sixteen percent. The study suggests to use cute objects to induce more care and focus in situations such as driving and office work.[20]

Many of us already use images in some form or another for motivation. Perhaps you have a portrait of your significant other, your children, or your dog on your desk to see you through the day. You may use a vision board to remind you of the reasons you work so hard. Additionally, use *kawaii* to your advantage as well. If you like animals, store some images of baby animals on your smart phone or laptop. If you have children, keep photos of them in their baby years handy. Anything that elicits a cute response from you will do the trick. Try it and see if it works.

Business Lesson

Use cute pictures of your pet, children, or fantasy characters to motivate you during the day. Research shows that this can improve your performance drastically.

Sort Out Your Workplace

The Japanese have a reputation for order and organization. They are masters of optimizing processes to increase their efficiency. The *Toyota Production System*, for example, has helped a small company known for shoddy products after the Second World War become the world leader in cars. Part of their process is a workplace organization method called *5S*,

---

[20] Plos One. The Power of Kawaii: Viewing Cute Images Promotes a Careful Behavior and Narrows Attentional Focus.
http://www.plosone.org/article/info%3Adoi%2F10.1371%2Fjournal.pone.0046362.

which stands for:[21]

- *Seiri:* Sort
- *Seiton:* Stabilize or set in order
- *Seiso:* Shine
- *Seiketsu:* Standardise
- *Shitsuke:* Sustain

The origins of the 5S methodology are in manufacturing, but it makes equal sense in any other business. *Sorting* involves removing unnecessary clutter. You should only keep the tools you need and get rid of things that are broken. Your tools should be stored neatly by *setting them in order*. They should be easy to find for you and others who may need them to save time and mental energy. Part of this is naming documents and files on your computer so that it is immediately clear what they are. *Shine* stands for keeping your workplace clean. You should have good light, best would be natural light. By *standardizing* the 5S policies you make sure that all staff knows how to apply and *sustain* them.

Everybody knows that order is important to put your time to effective use. How to go about sorting out your workplace, however, is often less clear. Try the 5S method and see if it helps you organize your desk or office and keep it that way.

Business Lesson

Your desk and workplace should be orderly and clean so you and others easily find the necessary tools and files. Standardize your method of organization so you can easily teach it to new members of your staff.

Get Up Early

Getting up early is a virtue for many Japanese. Sure, like everywhere else, there will also be those who sleep late and have trouble getting going in the morning. Nevertheless, on balance, successful individuals get up earlier than most others. Japanese students often wake up at 5 AM and study before

---

[21] Liker, Jeffrey K; The Toyota Way: 14 Management Principles from the World's Greatest Manufacturer. McGraw-Hill, 2004.

they start their school day. Several Japanese entrepreneurs I know visit the 24-hour driving range at dawn and practice their golf shots. Research has confirmed that people whose performance peaks in the morning are better positioned for career success because they are more proactive than people who are at their best in the evening.[22] The early bird really does catch the worm.

Getting up early may not work for everyone. Perhaps there are certain body types that simply need more sleep. Nobody I know particularly enjoys getting up early, myself included. However, I do enjoy getting things done. I love the feeling of accomplishment: Checking off half my to-do list before 8 AM gives me a big boost. This easily beats the first few minutes where I have to push myself when the alarm goes off. If you can handle it, I am sure you will feel an improvement in your productivity when you get up early. Set your alarm at 5 AM for a week and see if it works for you.

Business Lesson

Teach yourself to get up earlier. This habit can improve your productivity massively.

Work Hard, Play Hard

The Japanese often stay in the office until 8 PM, sometimes until 10 PM. They may not be working all the time, but still, they spend time away from their families, often without compensation. Work is a big part of people's identities. They define themselves through the company they work for and the job they do. No wonder that working hard is an asset that many Japanese are proud of. It also has its particular rewards, otherwise, I doubt they would find the motivation do get through the week.

Life in Japan is far from being all work and no play. If you have ever taken the subway in Tokyo late at night, you will have noticed the many inebriated "salary men" and "office ladies" who are on their way home after drinks with their co-workers. When you visit an *izakaya*, the Japanese word for "drinking place," the boozy and exuberant atmosphere at night can produce such noise that carrying a conversation is difficult. Parties on the weekend in Tokyo usually start around midnight and last until the sun

---

[22] Randler, Christoph. Harvard Business Review (HBR). Defend Your Research: The Early Bird Really Does Get the Worm. July 2010.
http://hbr.org/2010/07/defend-your-research-the-early-bird-really-does-get-the-worm/ar/1.

comes up, and concert audiences in Japan have a reputation as the most rambunctious anywhere on the planet.

Clearly, the Japanese take pride in working hard. But playing hard is of equal importance. Blowing off steam seems to give them back the equilibrium they so crave. After they went overboard on the weekend, showing up at the office on Monday morning with recharged batteries is easier.

Business Lesson

In times of intense workload, make sure you counterbalance with intense fun. Rewarding yourself is motivating, and it helps you to recharge your batteries.

CHAPTER 8: HOW TO SPOT AND AVOID TROUBLE

The most important part of dealing with challenges is avoiding them in the first place. You may know how to spot trouble in your established work environment. But in global projects, you need to have a better understanding of the different work cultures that come together. This can help you recognize and deal with sticky situations before they erupt into full-blown problems. Here are a few do's and don'ts that I picked up in Japan.

Understand the Mentality

We already talked about the low risk tolerance of most Japanese. Even decision makers often have trouble coming to a resolution, even though it is them who are supposed to steer the ship. More important than excelling at their job seems to be avoiding mistakes. This means they cover their own behind at every juncture. There are different ways to do this, and you should understand them when you want to avoid trouble. Let's examine a few of them here, along with techniques you can use to avoid trouble.

Herd Mentality

Many Japanese find safety in numbers. Their herd mentality has given them the reputation of a school of fish, a flock of sheep, who gladly follow their leader. If you break up the flock and try to force individual team members to work independently, you will run into trouble. Better assign tasks to small teams, even if they just consist of two people.

Avoiding to Rock the Boat

When decisions run the risk of rocking the boat, the Japanese will avoid them at all cost. They may even endorse those decisions secretly, but when it is up to them to deliver the bad news, they vote against them any day. If a situation is to the disadvantage of anyone on the team, they need a scapegoat who shoulders the blame. You as a foreigner are an ideal candidate. If you are in a leadership position with a slightly higher standing than the rest of the group, you may volunteer to stick your neck out. Make necessary decisions yourself and avoid delegating them to those of lower status than you.

The Opinion of Others

The Japanese are notoriously concerned with what others think of them. This goes far beyond the hierarchy in the workplace. The opinion of the boss matters, but so does the opinion of the intern. The reason is once more that they try to avoid any disruption to their precious harmony at the workplace. What exposes a person to the critique of others will create stress in the group. This is nothing you can cure by encouraging people to have more confidence. It is so deeply engrained that you better avoid exposing others. Better address sensitive issues in private with individual team members.

Business Lessons

When different cultures come together in a project, try to understand them. You need to navigate within the comfort zones of your colleagues and team members to avoid unnecessary tension and see your projects through successfully.

Accept Things Beyond Your Control

Modern Japan is largely free of the ethnic, religious and class divisions that characterize many other countries. The distance between rich and poor is much smaller, and almost ninety percent of the Japanese consider themselves middle class. In the past, strict social and economic separation existed between Japan's aristocracy and everybody else. The push for modernization in the Meiji period at the end of the 19th century and Allied occupation after WWII did much to bring down the rigid class system. Arranged marriages still exist, but most young Japanese women and men are free to make personal decisions related to their careers and their love life.

Despite encouraging individual empowerment, Japan's society remains heavily group-oriented. Children learn group consciousness in their families. As they grow up, membership in groups extends to their class in school, their neighborhood, sports clubs and the workplace. Forgoing personal gain for the benefit of these groups ranks high in the minds of the Japanese. Groups have strong hierarchies, where members have responsibilities that come with their status. Age plays a vital part in this, and young people learn to respect their seniors early on. I have seen Japanese workers apologize for mistakes by kneeling in front of a superior, bowing repeatedly and hanging their heads in shame. In the West, this might be considered abuse of authority in the workplace, but not so in Japan. Showing respect and deference outranks personal dignity still today.

When you work in Japan as a foreigner, you have a little more leeway. Being an exotic newcomer, you have a head start in the hierarchy above your Japanese peers. However, this will be short-lived. Unless you meet or exceed expectations, your status gradually dwindles and you find yourself at the bottom of the pyramid before you know it. Regardless where you are in the pecking order, you should always subordinate your opinion to those of your superiors and treat them with the utmost respect. Their standpoint has priority. Even if it is wrong, better nod and accept it instead of venturing into an argument that rocks the boat.

Japanese hierarchies have been around forever. It is tempting to believe you can influence how they work. When you want to do business in Japan, you need to accept that some things are out of your control. Find a way to live with them and use them to your own advantage.

Business Lesson

There will be things beyond your control in foreign cultures. Trying to change them is often a waste of time. Better find a way to accept them and use them to your advantage.

Avoid Direct Confrontation

Whenever possible, most Japanese avoid direct confrontation. They frown upon arguments in front of the team, blaming others publicly for their mistakes, or making people apologize to the group. Such things are often ineffective and unnecessary in the first place. Shaming tactics are a thing of the past. In modern management they have little use and merit.

When somebody has made a mistake, then avoid discussing it in public or gossiping about it. The Japanese have a proverb saying that gossip about a person will make his shadow appear. That is exactly what you should try to avoid. When you confront people directly and in front of others in Japan, you will create more problems than you solve. Better seek a personal conversation and bring up the issue indirectly. For example, if you suspect someone is slacking in their work, then you could ask the person in private how he or she suggest you deal with team members who fail to pull their weight. Then see what happens. Most importantly, you give the other person space to explain their shortcomings by themselves. They will often understand what you are trying to do and will offer to change their ways without your asking for it.

Complications will happen in any team. Confronting people directly in Japan will have two negative effects. First, it will rarely solve the issue. Second, you now also have to deal with the damage you caused by making people lose face. Better invent some indirect ways to express your dissatisfaction. This will save you much headache and get you better results.

Business Lesson

Some business cultures avoid direct confrontation at all costs. If this is the case, voice your dissatisfaction indirectly with team members on a one-on-one basis. Find indirect ways to address issues and give the other person enough space to explain.

Let Others Deliver Bad News

A little earlier, when we talked about understanding business mentality in Japan, we learned that the Japanese are eager to save face. It is therefore natural to assume that we as foreigners who should carry the load to protect the Japanese team. This is of course the easiest solution, however, it can turn out to be to your disadvantage in the long run. Even though saving face may mean little more to you than a phrase, you should make sure the Japanese respect you. You need to protect your image and reputation, and you should avoid being the fall guy per default.

Better than making yourself available as the scapegoat, use the system to your advantage, just like the Japanese. Look for someone else who can deliver bad news, give disruptive orders, or admonish those who performed below expectations. For you, the natural thing to do is look up. If possible, find a Japanese superior who you enlist to carry out these tasks on your behalf. Once more, you need to ask for this indirectly. Otherwise, the task will land right back in your court. Ask for your superior's opinion about a certain issue. You may choose to make it look like you failed to notice the shortcoming and let him uncover it himself. Then it is up to him to deal with it.

Business Lesson

"Saving face" is important in some cultures, both for locals and foreigners. Make sure you offload anything with the potential to result in your loss of face. For critical issues, ideal candidates are those higher up the food chain.

Look for Red Flags

Making a project work in Japan is definitely more difficult than doing the same elsewhere. Unless you grew up in Japan and speak the language perfectly, the odds are against you. For this reason you should stack the deck in your favor. This is what we are attempting all the while with the business lessons in this book. However, knowing what to *do* is only one side of the coin. The other is knowing what to *avoid*. If you do everything right but keep exposing yourself to unnecessary risks, your chances of success may still be marginal.

Some things are twisted in Japan. A great movie called *Audition* tells such a twisted tale.[23] The story goes like this: The son of a middle-aged widower urges him to begin dating again. One of the widower's friends, a film producer, fakes a casting audition in which young actresses apply for the mock part of his new wife. One girl immediately catches his attention. None of the references on her resume check out, but he still pursues her. A series of twists and turns later, we learn that she harbors a dark secret. Without giving away the ending, it is safe to say that things end badly for the widower. Even though he had plenty of indications that something was wrong, he chose to override his gut feeling and paid a heavy price.

When you feel something is wrong, then stop, and listen to your gut. It always tells you when you are about to make a mistake or take on an unnecessary risk. If there are any red flags in a project, please take them seriously. In Japan, you need to be extra careful. Because everything seems to different, it is easy to rationalize risks away. Nevertheless, you need to be comfortable with the people you work with and the deals you sign. This holds true in Japan as much as anywhere else.

---

[23] Wikipedia. Audition (オーディション, Odishon, 1999). Takashi Miike (director). http://en.wikipedia.org/wiki/Audition_%281999_film%29.

Business Lesson

Just as important as making the right choices is avoiding the wrong ones. Learn to listen to your gut feeling and pay attention to red flags. Unless you are comfortable with people, situations and deals, better stay away.

Stay Legal

What is perfectly legal in one country may be a felony in another. Even within the code of law, countries have their own priorities which ones they enforce before others. Europe, for example, has a relatively lax policy on enforcing drug possession. Japan, on the other hand, runs a tight ship in this regard. Carrying even small amounts of certain herbal medicine, used for recreational purposes, results in high fines and hard time in jail. Can you run a successful business project out of a jail cell? When you have run-ins with the law, your dream of making it big abroad is usually over.

This happened to a friend of mine, a graffiti artist from New York. A gallery in Tokyo had invited him for a solo exhibition. For the occasion of the art show, they printed a book of his murals and invited luminaries of Tokyo pop culture as well as distinguished members of the press. However, on the day of the opening, the artist was nowhere to be seen. He failed to show up at the art gallery, and the entire event took place without him. A week later he called from jail. As graffiti artists do, he felt he needed to grace the city with his art the night before the show. Police had caught him when he was spray-painting in Shibuya. Unaware that the men trying to apprehend him were undercover officers, he swung his backpack filled with spray cans at one of them and broke the guy's nose. Spray tagging is a crime, but his charge had escalated to assault and battery of a police officer. This is no laughing matter in Japan, and it ended in a stiff fine and three months in jail. This was his first and last visit to the country.

If you are serious about your projects, avoid any clashes with the law and the authorities. Even if you believe you are smart and will not be caught, the law in a foreign country is rarely on your side. It is easy to believe that the stories in the press happen to others but not to you. When they happen, they come with grave consequences. The same goes for the company you keep. Better mingle with other professionals who are dedicated to running successful businesses than those who gamble with their future. There are enough legal means to have fun. Stick with those to save yourself a lot of trouble.

Business Lesson

Avoid illegal actions and brushes with the law. Starting a company and working abroad is already difficult enough. Better save yourself the added stress of having to deal with the authorities or defending yourself in court.

Charity Undermines Leadership

You may know the saying that "no good deed shall go unpunished." This roughly means that by trying to do something good, you often end up in trouble. The Japanese have no similar proverb that I am aware of. When I tried to explain its meaning, most of my friends in Japan did not understand what this quote meant. Still, it is just as important to keep in mind in Japan like anywhere else.

We already learned that you need any help you can get when you do business in Japan, part of which is avoiding unnecessary risks. One way to do this is staying away of trying to be a hero. Now what exactly does this mean? You may be in a position where you hire local staff for your Japanese project. One of cute girls you hired suggests that her sister would make a perfect candidate for position XYZ. This is exactly where you should draw the line. Instead of doling out favors and in the process attracting the suspicion of favoritism, adhere to your established hiring practices. The same applies to being generous by inviting your staff on nights out. You may think that you collect goodwill this way but, unfortunately, being nice will rarely help you establish authority. If you are in a position of leadership, do things like a Japanese boss would. This book has already given you some pointers in this direction.

Make sure you avoid blurring the line between business and private relationships. Once your co-workers get the feeling that you are an easygoing boss, a meal-ticket, or – even worse – that you sleep around with your staff, you will have a hard time commanding their respect when it matters. This will only show when there is an emergency or the project takes an unfavorable turn. In sticky situations, you need credit to rule with authority. If you were soft before, trying to bring about a change in your perception in a crisis will be impossible.

This is far from suggesting that you run your project like a military commander. However, find a balance and separate business from fun and games and charity. Regardless of your position in the food chain, you need your colleagues to respect you. Do this by making smart decisions, not by buying others or doling out favors.

Business Lesson

When you work abroad, locals may see you as a wildcard where established rules do not apply. Especially when you are in a position of leadership, you need authority. Avoid trying to gain it with acts of charity. No good deed shall go unpunished.

If Something Looks Complicated, Improvise

When you care about making a good impression, compliance with the rules can take up a lot of your time and energy. With its convoluted corporate culture and its countless informal rules for private and professional behavior, Japan is easily one of the most complex places to do business in. To preserve your resources, you need to understand the rules. But only those that are truly important. Use the 80/20 principle to separate the wheat from the chaff. It is often the twenty percent of things that are relatively easy to do that yield eighty percent of the results. Mastering the most complicated rules often contributes so little that the effort is rarely worth it. When they do come up, cross your fingers and improvise.

I had been invited to visit a shrine in the countryside with the family of a business partner. In Tokyo, I had already been to many of the large temples and shrines, so I was vaguely familiar with the procedures. But this time would be different. This shrine was a modest building in a private garden of around 10,000 square feet (1,000 square meters), which belonged to the family. The structure was so small that only one person at a time could kneel in front of it, lay down some flowers, light incense and say a prayer. This was a traditional Japanese family with their own elaborate protocol for the visit, and I was told that no other foreigner had ever stepped on this sacred ground.

The business partner had tried to teach me a traditional Japanese prayer that filled an entire page in a book. I heard other family members say it at the shrine, but it was too long and too complex to recall. Obviously, they wanted me to do everything right. When it was my turn, I solemnly walked up to the shrine, kneeled down, assumed a prayer position and closed my eyes for thirty seconds. When they asked me later what I had been praying for, I mentioned that I was recalling that family prayer, but in my own words in English. Of course this was stretching the truth, but it was enough to make everybody happy.

In Japan, it matters often more that you *try* to do something right than actually doing it right. Especially as a foreigner, you will have enormous leeway if you make an effort to grasp the culture and blend in. Some Japanese will have difficulty to understand that certain customs are extremely hard to do for foreigners. Instead of trying to explain the reasons, better just go with the flow and fly by the seat of your pants. This often deflects situations with a high chance of escalating into something uncomfortable.

Business Lesson

When situations become overly complex, simplify and improvise instead of trying to do everything right. Address cultural conventions with the 80/20 rule by focusing on those things that yield the highest results. It is often safe to forget about the rest.

How to Deal with Discrimination

Unfortunately, the Japanese have a reputation for being intolerant of foreigners, immigrants, racial minorities and those with different viewpoints. One should never generalize, of course. I have experienced most Japanese people as open-minded and welcoming. Nevertheless, racial discrimination against other Asians was frequent in Imperial Japan, having begun with the start of Japanese colonialism.[24] Before and after the Second World War, crimes and pogroms against ethnic minorities and foreigners were wide-spread. Today, the constitution of Japan states that all people or citizens are equal under the law. They cannot be discriminated against politically, economically, or socially on the basis of race, belief, sex, social or any other background. However, Japan still lacks civil rights legislation to enforce or penalize discrimination.[25]

Personally, I never suffered from discrimination. If it happened, then I was not aware of it. However, indirect comments are quite frequent, for example jokes and remarks in passing about foreigners or certain minorities

---

[24] Bix, Herbert. Hirohito and the Making of Modern Japan. Harper-Collins, 2000.
[25] Wikipedia. Ethnic Issues in Japan.
http://en.wikipedia.org/wiki/Ethnic_issues_in_Japan.

or groups. When things go wrong, I have seen some Japanese resort to the easiest accuse of all: That the culprit is a foreigner with a different value system who will never know any better. This will rarely excuse a blunder, but start a domino effect that is the beginning of the end of a project or work relationship. Once a reputation is damaged, rightfully or not, chances for recovery are slim. For this reason, foreigners in Japan often stick together. Koreans do business with other Koreans, and so do the Chinese. This shields them against racial discrimination and keeps their business relations intact against false accusations. But when you work with Japanese business partners, it will be hard to completely shield yourself from potential discrimination. You need other coping strategies. Here are a few I have found helpful.

Speak up against negative jokes about foreigners or minorities

Point out that you find discriminatory remarks offensive, regardless if they target you or someone else. If you prefer to protest indirectly, excuse yourself, get up and leave the conversation.

Refrain from retaliation

It is easy to hit back when someone attacks you. When you take the high road, the attacker often shoots himself in the foot. Use peer pressure to your advantage. When you have done nothing wrong and are accused on false grounds, the attacker looks silly in the eyes of others and will think twice the next time around.

Be a role model

Refrain from negative comments about minorities or those who think different. When others display direct or indirect discrimination or racism, distance yourself from their behavior and the group. You can have your own opinion, but steer clear of making it public when it may discriminate others.

Discrimination is a worldwide phenomenon and by no means limited to Japan. In some cases, you may find yourself the victim of prejudice. Trying to prove your worth will rarely solve the problem. Better eject yourself from situations where you are at an unfair disadvantage from the start. Look for those you like you and help you to succeed. Otherwise, you may find yourself fighting a battle you cannot win.

Business Lesson

When you witness or are a victim of discrimination, speak up. Avoid confrontation and instead seek out those who like to do business with you on equal grounds. Refrain from discriminating others. This is against the law in many countries and can land you in hot water.

The Yakuza is Real

No book about Japan is complete without mentioning the *yakuza*, the Japanese mafia. Computer games and movies paint a romantic picture of this criminal organization. This makes it easy to forget that the yakuza is involved in protection rackets, human trafficking, drug trade and gambling. They also take part in legitimate businesses, such as banks and insurance companies. Ironically, Kobe, the home city of the largest yakuza syndicate Yamaguchi-gumi, is one of the safest cities in Japan. The reason is that low-level criminals like street gangs and thugs are afraid to attract the yakuza's attention so they go elsewhere.

Foreigners are often under the impression that yakuza are cool. Part of this may be their elaborate tattoos, which some Westerners emulate. However, remember that most gang members are convicted felons and killers. In reality, these guys are far removed from the whimsical characters that actor/director Takeshi Kitano plays in his yakuza dramas. Their profit is a direct result of somebody else's hardship. The yakuza are not small fish, either: Total gang membership hit 81,000 in 2009.[26]

A friend of mine (we met him earlier, the Japanese software entrepreneur) comes from a yakuza family. I quizzed him repeatedly about this association. Per his account, when a business makes one million US dollars and more in profit per year, it gets on the radar of the yakuza and a local thug will show up on its doorstep. A common racket is to demand protection money. Small business owners may have to give up twenty percent and more of their earnings for this purpose. If they refuse, there will be a fire or other calamity.

Regardless of what anybody says, the entire entertainment business in

---

[26] Corkill, Edan. Ex-Tokyo cop speaks out on a life fighting gangs. Tokyo Times, November 6, 2011. http://www.japantimes.co.jp/life/2011/11/06/life/ex-tokyo-cop-speaks-out-on-a-life-fighting-gangs-and-what-you-can-do/.

Japan is in yakuza hands. In some of the concert venues in Tokyo where I performed, there was armed security in the parking garage, guarding white Maybachs and Lamborghinis with number plates like "One" or "007." I met with some of these guys, too. They had generally interesting stories to tell. I had been introduced to a talent agency in Tokyo who represented famous Japanese pop stars and actors. This company wanted to take on a project that I worked on. It was one of those deals where I would sign over all rights to them, but in exchange, the profits that they generated through their business relationships would make it worthwhile. Such deal terms made me feel deeply uncomfortable. Once you are in bed with organized crime, there is no way out. Perhaps my projects would have been more successful had I not had this reservation. At least I can proudly say that I my vest is clean, for whatever that is worth. I recommend you do the same. When something is obviously criminal, better stay away.

Business Lesson

Gangsters have become role models in video games and movies but organized crime has a dark side. In some countries, professional gangs run large parts of the economy. Better avoid any connection with people who are obviously criminal. You will be able to sleep better at night.

CHAPTER 9: DAMAGE CONTROL

Sometimes it is too late to avert a calamity and it hits you full-frontal like a tsunami. Luckily, Japanese people have many strategies to salvage situations. Most of them are similar with those of the West, but the more unique techniques are what we are interested in here. They are direct results of my doing business in Japan but they also work elsewhere, especially when you need to make sure you deflect the blame, keep composed, and come out on top in an elegant way.

The Gaijin Twist

The Japanese call foreigners *gaijin*, which means "outside person." In recent years, the term has become somewhat controversial, and most Japanese television broadcasters now avoid it.[27] Some people believe it has negative overtones, others see the term as neutral. Whatever may be the case, a gaijin is someone who is normally not familiar with the rules of Japanese protocol and politeness. This can work to your advantage. Let's examine how.

Assume there is a major crisis in your project. A delivery has missed the mark by a huge margin, and the Japanese client is unhappy. Key personnel has threatened to leave, the team is disintegrating, a blame game has erupted, and the future of the entire project is on the rocks. Someone needs to explain the state of affairs to the incensed client. The Japanese will try to deflect the situation with overly polite behavior and submissive apologies. If this strategy fails to work, they are out of options. Here is where you come in. As a gaijin, you can go in the other direction: If you raise your voice, pound your fist on a desk, or even grab a chair and throw it through the office, no Japanese will be able to keep up with you. By becoming angry you can save someone else's face by concentrating the heat on you. The Japanese can blame it on the crazy foreigner and have something to bond between them. When a critical situation is at an impasse, this may stir it up and help it become unstuck.

You need to think for yourself if this ploy is something you want risk. Obviously, it could cost you your job, or it may even worsen a situation. On the other hand, if there is no other way out, then your gaijin status can be an asset. Because of your special standing, you can say things others would never dare, which can sometimes pull back a situation from the brink of disaster.

---

[27] Wikipedia. Gaijin. http://en.wikipedia.org/wiki/Gaijin.

Business Lesson

When a situation is at an impasse, most people seek a solution by deflecting the problem. As an outsider, you can go in the other direction: Stirring things up by doing something out of the ordinary may help the situation become unstuck.

Assume the Blame

Heads must roll in Japan when things have turned ugly. Client often forgives blunders as a result. Obviously, taking a hit goes at the expense of a person's status. If he or she repeatedly admits failure, chances for promotions dwindle and a downgrade in the corporate hierarchy follows. Even though Japanese workers are rarely fired, a low status is something they need to avoid.

As an outsider, especially when you work as a consultant on short-term projects, a temporary blow to your standing will rarely hurt your business prospects. Japanese people rely on a company's good graces for life-long employment and have no such luxury. Their number one priority is to save face and cover their own behind, they will be hesitant to sacrifice themselves to appease a client.

Once more, this is where you come in. When it is the only way out, assume all blame, even if you only had a small part in the failure of the project. When no one else sticks out their neck, this may save a project. Your Japanese colleagues and team members will thank you for it. However, be careful that this can also set a precedent for future situations. Be selective with your offers to be the scapegoat. Otherwise you end up in the corner by default.

Business Lesson

You may save a troubled project by assuming the blame for its failure. Especially if you have goodwill to cash in and can absorb a temporary blow to your status in the corporate hierarchy, this can often solve problems very quickly.

Let Others Vent Their Anger, But Be Overly Polite

When a project is floundering, most Japanese will tolerate harsh criticism by their irate clients. This is part of their strategy to deflect sticky situations. They avoid any argument and simply agree with all the accusations the client may have.

Together with my Japanese colleagues I sat through such meetings that sometimes lasted for hours. Instead of analyzing the situation rationally, clients would simply vent their unfiltered anger. Listening to verbal abuse is easier said than done, especially when the client is partly to blame for a mishap. In Europe or America, clients express their disappointment in a few sentences, and then it is up to the other person to explain and offer solutions. Not so in Japan. You may have to sit through hours of insults, all the while keeping your cool, lowering your head, and repeating how sorry you are. This is hard. But it is also often enough to make a problem go away.

Business Lesson

Instead of getting into arguments and blame games, let angry clients vent their anger to deflect a sticky situation. When they feel you heard their complaints, they are often more cooperative in finding constructive solutions.

How to Save Face, Yours and Others'

Loosely translated, "saving face" means that people try to avoid putting others on the spot by directly confronting them. They steer clear of situations where someone ends up with his back against the wall. When things turn bad, people think twice before they do anything that results in a loss of face. We already learned how to approach situations indirectly. This is exactly what saving face consists of.

Your first reaction to trouble should be to defer, deflect or absorb it. Instead of getting angry, contain the damage. Let's say you walk up to the refrigerator in your office and notice a puddle of water around it. It is obvious that someone has left the door open, which caused the ice in the freezer to melt. Instead of looking for the culprit and making him or her clean up the mess, rally the troops to contain the water. Send someone to find out if any of it has made its way through the ceiling down into the neighbors' offices. You could even exaggerate the situation and suggest that a pipe may have broken. Sooner or later, a Japanese person will suggest that it is simply a matter of an improperly shut refrigerator. Act surprised and suggest that the door or its seal may be at fault and start investigating it. Do you see how this works? Deflect the situation immediately away from the problem. Make it look as if it were an accident and nobody's fault. The culprit will know at this point. He may come forward or not. But one thing is clear: He will take extra care when taking something out of the fridge the next time.

Thinking in terms of saving face rarely comes natural to people from the West. I had to learn this in Japan over several years. However, deflection techniques are valuable whenever you work in teams. Make saving face a habit, both in Asia and beyond, to address situations more effectively and elegantly.

Business Lesson

Deflect attention away from a problem to its solution. Instead of trying to identify the culprit, better give him or her space to realize the mistake and come forward. This makes you look like a superior leader and not a finger pointer.

Promise to Solve the Problem, No Matter What

In Japan, the leader assumes all responsibility when the team has made a mistake. He promises to see to it that the project goes through according to plan in the future. Even if the mistake lies with the client, true leadership means taking the blame. The only thing that matters is that things go smoothly in the time ahead, not who is at fault. With this focus on the future, the Japanese like to concentrate on describing the outcome of projects in glowing terms. However, explaining how exactly this will happen is secondary. I have seen executives make wild promises that were clearly unrealistic. What mattered was that the client got the impression everything was under control. Any challenge would be solved, no matter what. Projecting control and stability is sometimes more important than having a detailed roadmap.

On the other hand, it is true that the Japanese like to plan things meticulously. Organization is one of their key strengths. However, those in leadership positions also know when to switch to a different modus operandi. Flying by the seats of their pants is rarely part of the curriculum in management schools, nevertheless, good leaders have this skill in their toolkit. If you find yourself in a position of responsibility, prepare yourself to improvise from time to time. Promise to deliver results without knowing how exactly they will come about. If you fail, then at least you tried all you could. If you pull it off, you are a hero.

Business Lesson

Promise to deliver results, no matter what it will take. Assure the client that you know what to do, even though you may need to improvise. In the end, how you achieved a result is less important than achieving it in the first place.

Pull Yourself Together

We already learned a few techniques to solve problems in Japan. If you see them for the first time, they may seem to you like making yourself small and weak in front of your clients. It may look like this on the surface, but in Japan, the humble are the strong. Fighting back and getting into arguments is a sign of weakness. For this reason, the Japanese consider much of the Western behavior to cope with a crisis as flawed. For example, placing the blame on someone else, lying and finding an excuse, or arguing that there is no mistake in the first place will seldom go over well. Instead, accepting the blame, working hard to find a solution, and helping everybody save face are signs of true strength. Unless you are superhuman, this will require a lot of strength and effort.

The underlying principle in Japanese problem solving is that you should always look like you know how to handle the situation. Even when things become extremely stressful and you feel that you are at a breaking point, never show weakness. Never admit that you are unsure how to deal with a challenge. This will destroy your reputation in an instant. Remember: The strong have no problem apologizing and accepting blame. Those who are weak will look for the easy way out.

Scripted protocols dictate the ways the Japanese are supposed to act and respond in difficult situations. Perhaps these rules are so ingrained that their behavior becomes automatic. However, solving problems the Japanese way demanded a lot of my energy. When I found myself in unjust situations and felt the anger rise inside me, I needed to make a conscious effort to pull myself together. Without it, I would have blurted out the wrong responses, made blunders even worse, and insulted people beyond the chance of repair.

When doing business in Japan, toughen up. Learn to bite your lip and improvise while making everything look effortless. This sounds incredibly simple and easy to agree with while you read it in a book. When you start carrying out this advice, you will see what it takes. Welcome situations where you can practice this skill. It will come in handy in more situations than you can imagine.

Business Lesson

Develop a thick skin and pull yourself together. When things are hard, avoid the easy way out. Instead, use the situation to learn how to deal with it more effectively. This will make you mentally stronger and a better business person.

Give Them Something

You should always aim to delight and impress your clients, both in Japan and elsewhere. Nevertheless, there may be situations where everything goes wrong. The project is teetering on the brink of falling apart, and the clients threatens legal action. As we just learned, the Japanese will rarely enter into arguments here. Still, the client may feel he suffered damage and needs more than simple apologies.

If delivering what you promised turns out to be impossible, then at least give *something* to your client. If they feel they have a small win, they may take the heat off. This often means they will renegotiate the deal. It may turn out the deadline was less firm than the client made you believe, and you can deliver later. If they get at least some appreciation from you, they may accommodate you in return.

A few years ago, a news story about a Japanese music manager made the rounds. He had cheated a well-known heavy metal band for the equivalent of about half a million dollars and then vanished. This is as far as the press reported the tale, the interesting part took place off the record. A member of this band later told me that the manager reached out to them a week after his disappearance. He apologized and organized a lucrative placement of one of their songs in a TV commercial. In exchange, he demanded that they drop all charges against him. So they did. They dropped the case and stopped pressing for repayment, he apologized and brought them a high-income project. Both parties found a compromise, none of them lost face. A classic Japanese solution.

If they made a blunder, Japanese people apologize and offer something in return. This will often clear the debt, set the stage for renegotiations, and resume the project as if nothing happened.

Business Lesson

When you made a blunder and fail to deliver, offer the client at least something. This establishes goodwill for renegotiations, and you may see the project through under new and better deal terms.

Never Pay Back Money

The result of a failed project is often a financial loss for the client. Especially if you received payment upfront (which I hope you did), the client can clearly specify his loss. Our natural instinct is often to offer to pay back money or complete the rest of the project at a discount. In Japan, this is much less common than elsewhere. Small businesses rarely have liability insurance, and the bank accounts of entrepreneurs or more often overdrawn than bulging with venture capital. Most of the advance fee has already found its way into payments for overhead or salaries for third parties.

Renegotiations during the course of projects are very common in Japan, however, paying back money is out of the question. You set the price at the beginning, and this is what you should stick to. If you suddenly lower your fee, it sends the wrong message. To the client, it looks like you overcharged him in the first place. If you can also complete the project at a lower fee, then why did you ask for more? If there is any repeat business, you will find yourself stuck at the lower price forever. Another reason is that as soon as you pay back your advance, the project is usually over. You have lost money and a client. Better keep the project alive and do all you can to turn it around.

When you made a mistake, offer to deliver something extra. Go the extra mile and bump up the project in priority. Spend more time on it, or allocate better resources to it. If you sell a product to a client, deliver fifty percent more for the same price. If it is a service, give your client the VIP treatment. I learned this lesson in Japan and have used it everywhere else since.

Business Lesson

When you made a mistake, never pay back advances or lower the price. Competing by price is something you need to avoid. Better deliver extra product or a higher quality of service. This may save the project and you gained a client for the long term.

CHAPTER 10: MY MAIN TAKEAWAYS

In the three years I lived and worked in Tokyo, I learned more than in most of my time as an entrepreneur before. As you may have guessed, many of my adventures were hard and frustrating, others were among the best I have had in my life so far. Looking back, some of the lessons I learned stand out. When I tried to assign them to a chapter, I noticed they were harder to classify because they spanned disciplines and summarized several business lessons. For this reason, my main takeaways deserved a chapter on their own. Even though I use all the business lessons in this book in my work outside of Japan, they reverberate the most.

Agree to Disagree

Even though you might not particularly love Japanese animation and movies, you will agree that there is something special and fascinating about them. The way people speak, walk and act is distinctly different from your own culture. Once I read up on their history, I got the feeling that Japanese culture was almost alien, perhaps far ahead of ours. Maybe this is the reason that so many people from the West study the language or Japan studies at universities. However, it has become clear throughout this book that blending in with the Japanese ways is no cakewalk. Both their business culture and their personal beliefs are often at odds with those of the West, which can lead to much confusion and energy drain.

When something is fascinating, it can be exhausting to keep up with. Trying to blend in and seeking approval on a daily basis takes a lot of mental energy. About a year into my stay I gave up trying to do everything right. I did what I could to honor the culture and traditions, but I made little effort to perfectly master the language or emulate the Japanese ways in everything I did. Agreeing to disagree became my motto. This applied to how far I chose to blend in and also how far I defended my own standpoint. It helped me establish a reputation as a respectful colleague, but one who did certain things his own way. With this, much of the energy drain stopped, and life in Japan became easier and more fun.

Business Lesson

You may feel you want to immerse yourself completely in a new culture, but this can become exhausting to keep up with. Agree to disagree in those points that cost you too much energy. Learn to blend different perspectives together. This can enrich both the foreign culture and your own.

Outsider Advantages

At first sight, it seemed to me like there were only disadvantages to being an outsider in Japan. Luckily, I recognized that this was a limiting belief. *Because* I was an outsider, I was able to carve out advantages for myself that natives could only dream of. When I understood that being a fish out of the water came with bonuses beyond doing business, pursuing my goals came more natural. Things became more fun and I learned to mix and match the experiences that I had acquired in my previous adventures in Asia, Europe and America.

Even those expats who lived in Japan for decades report of their journey with one eye laughing and one eye crying. They love the culture and the people, but they struggle with the feeling exclusion, with no chance of ever fully belonging to this fascinating tribe. Even though they may have a Japanese spouse and children, those Japanese who see them for the first time still brand them as a lowly gaijin. The will always be an outsider.

The Western business culture first seemed to be an obstacle to working in Japan. We have seen foreigners made fools of themselves throughout this book. However, those who find a balance between different cultures have an advantage. By complying with the rules, they seem calm outwardly, but inwardly, they are unencumbered and think on your feet. Oppressive cultural norms only apply to them on the outside, while they can do and think whatever they want when nobody is looking. Especially for entrepreneurs this is a plus. It looks like they do nothing out of the ordinary, until the competition has lost market share to them and wakes up too late to take them seriously.

Knowing different cultures gives you options to choose from. Like a computer with several operating systems, you pick what works best for each individual application. You know what works in both worlds and can mix and match. But this advantage is only yours if you make an effort to understand new local traditions and their rules. Learning the ropes is often well worth the trouble.

Business Lesson

Being an outsider comes with advantages. You get special credit for being exotic and different and a higher status in corporate hierarchy at the beginning. Most importantly, you are fluent in different cultures at the same time. This can become your secret weapon.

Life Is Short

There is a minor earthquake somewhere in Japan every day, often so faint that you hardly notice it before it is over. Because it became difficult to distinguish whether the ground really shook beneath my feet or I just imagined it, I made habit of placing a half-full glass of water on my desk. Whenever the surface of the water became restless, I knew there was a quake in progress.

I had experienced tremors in Los Angeles and in Tokyo before, so I knew what to do in case of an emergency. But my experience paled compared to what happened on March 11 in 2011. I had just finished lunch at my apartment in Tokyo and was washing my hands in the bathroom. All of a sudden, the door swung open. Before I could wrap my head around what was going on, the whole place started shaking. OK, I thought, here we go again. I made my way into the kitchen and placed the dishes that I just wanted to wash on the floor so they would not fall down. The quake should be over any second. However, the room was like a boat at sea. Chairs tipped over, the flat screen TV crashed to the floor, kitchen cabinets flung open and a spice rack that came flying out hit me on the head. A deep growling noise like a large animal added to the spooky atmosphere. The quake did not seem to end, even though it only lasted minutes. I was crouching under the table and waited it out. The apartment was on the eleventh floor. I wondered what it would be like if the walls came loose and the floor fell out under me. The thought occurred to me that this might be the end. I had never felt death so near like on this day.

All of a sudden, the shaking stopped, as if someone had stepped on the breaks and a car came to a standstill. When the worst seemed to be over, I inspected the damage. The place looked like someone had turned it upside down, but there seemed to be no structural damage to the building. My cell phone still worked, so I turned on the TV (yes, you can watch TV on the Japanese cell phone network). The earthquake had been a 9.0 on the Richter scale, one the most violent ever measured. Now the news showed pictures of the sea that was strangely withdrawing in the coastal regions of Japan. Half an hour later, I watched the worst tsunami in history in real time. By evening, the news broke that the power plant in Fukushima was at risk of a nuclear meltdown. This area was just 200 kilometers away. My embassy send me an email. Because of the impending nuclear apocalypse, they relocated to the Westside of Japan and offered to fly all their citizens out of the country in a chartered jet. They also sent iodine tablets against radiation poisoning and suggested I take one right away. At the same time, the Japanese news reported there was no danger at all. I was scared to leave the apartment.

After two days of shacking up at home, I had eaten through my stash of top ramen and snacks and had to do something to procure food. Carefully, I ventured to a 7Eleven a block away. All its shelves were wiped clean and it was closed. There was almost no one outside. The city looked deserted like in a zombie movie. Another supermarket still had some food, mainly foreign snacks, chocolate and sweets. Rice, vegetables and meat were sold out. So were all instant meals, cup noodles and frozen foods. There was no drinking water or any other bottled beverage available. I bought what I could and went home. Almost every hour, there were aftershocks, but none as violent as the main quake.

I spend a week glued to the TV on phone, waiting for a signal that things were safe. Then life went back to normal on the surface. People reported back to work and supermarkets stocked up on normal food again. The Fukushima situation was still in the air, but at least we had water and something to eat. Foreign news media pieced together the truth about the molten reactor. The water supply of some areas of Tokyo had been contaminated. I am pretty sure I drank radioactive tap water for a few days.

Just as this disaster shook Japan to the core, it seemed to stir me up as well. I had been in Tokyo for three years. After my initial project came to an end, I ventured out on several new ones on my own, but they were mainly loss leaders. Without noticing it, Tokyo had become a convenient bubble. I could stay there for years longer, travel, study, and have a comfortable life, but what good would this be if I never sharpened my senses in the real world? The earthquake was my wake-up call. It motivated me to examine the choices in my life and my career, which convinced me I needed to expand my horizon with new skills that would be valuable in the future. A new urgency had captivated me, a sensation that life was short. Before the end of the month, I packed my bags and left the country for good.

Business Lesson

Examine the direction of your life from time to time. You may find that you are stuck in a comfortable rut. When this is the case, make a change. Life is short and you need to make the most of it while you can.

EPILOGUE: BEYOND JAPAN

Now you know more about practical Japanese business culture than most graduates in Japan studies and international MBAs. The business lessons in this book are of the kind that you will rarely find in academic studies about Japanese management or etiquette books. No two people are alike and I am certain that others with the same experiences in Japan as me would draw their own conclusions. The strength of the lessons in this book is that they are personal. They are the results of my personal experiences, and by writing them down, I feel I shared with you an important part of my life in Japan.

Chances are you are working in Japan or are planning to do so in the near future. Nevertheless, even if you never set foot in that country, what we discussed in this book is valid for your work as an employee, manager or entrepreneur anywhere in the world. If you live in Asia, many of the Japanese ways will sound familiar to you. In Western countries, look at them as metaphors. As always, knowing how other people tackle situations and challenges may give you ideas for new approaches of your own. Thinking about situations from fresh angles will help you find unexpected solutions, and taking a peek at them through the Japanese lens helps you gain distance and perspective.

Even though I no longer live in Japan, I still use most of these business lessons in my projects today. Tackling situations with new strategies is always helpful. So is combining several techniques. I encourage you experiment with the information in this book. As with any business advice, the only thing that matters is for you to take action. *How* we do something is often more important than *what* we do. First and foremost, I wanted to inspire you with this book to reflect on things in a different light. If you go out and test something you have read here, I have achieved my goal.

おわり

APPENDIX: A PRIMER ON JAPAN

In case you're relatively new to Japan, let's get some background information about its history and its people. This will help us put some of the customs and curiosities into perspective. Otherwise, they might seem like strange habits that the Japanese have chosen to acquire. In reality, most of what characterizes Japan today is rooted in its history.

Short History Recap

Several events in the last hundred years built the foundation of modern Japan. Bear with me here for a few minutes, this information will make many of the business lessons that follow later appear much clearer.

The Meiji Restoration

Until the late nineteenth century, Japan was a relatively unassuming group of islands. Feudal lords ruled its agricultural society. It was during the Meiji restoration (1886-1912) when the development started that shaped the country into a modern economy. Japan had shut itself off from the world for centuries, but closing the gap to the advanced countries was now a question of national survival. To accomplish this, the Japanese copied the attributes of a modern society into their traditional framework. A new administrative and legal system gave the ruling class more effective instruments of power. Education underwent a reform with a concentration on science and engineering, and the state heavily promoted industrial development and encouraged the import of advanced technologies from the West. A close working relationship grew up between the bureaucrats of the administration and the family concerns that came to dominate the modern sectors of the economy. Mostly invisible, a tiny minority still remains in charge of business and industry in Japan today.

From Agriculture to an Industrial Society

By the First World War (1914-1918), Japan had imposed an imperialist policy on its Asian neighbors. However, despite rapid growth in industrial production, its output of steel, coal and consumer goods still lagged behind advanced Western countries. Living standards were still low, and state policy largely benefitted the already rich and powerful. Japanese consumers were frugal and saved a lot. Traditional features of society, such as close-knit family ties, the dependence of women on fathers and husbands, and the obedience to social superiors, enabled the Japanese miracle. Even though similar traits exist in societies which are still backward, the Japanese were eager to absorb overseas knowledge and employed imported expertise to help found new industries. At the same time, they carefully avoided dependence and maintained their own culture. The Japanese always kept foreigners at arm's length while they extracted the maximum from business deals with them.

Economic Effects of the World Wars

When Japan expanded its territory in China after WWI, its war-related industries began to grow rapidly. Small- and medium-sized factories carried out large parts of domestic production still using manual labor. As a result, Japanese goods were of low quality, which lead to their bad reputation abroad. Industrialization was picking up but was still immature.

Fast forward twenty years. Defeated in WWII in 1945, Japan now found itself under allied occupation. The economy lay in shambles. Food and raw materials were running low and inflation was rampant. However, war defeat and occupation represented a turning point in Japanese history almost on a par with the Meiji Restoration. As a counterweight to the communist bloc, American interests required an economically viable Japan. Borrowing foreign technology had always been characteristic of Japanese progress, but now, the field for profitable investment in Japan seemed unlimited.

Recovering from two wars, the world entered a boom period after 1950, from which Japan profited as the workshop of the world. A short thirty years later, when the American automotive industry suffered losses, Japan had become the world's largest motor vehicle manufacturer. Japanese products did not sell on cheapness any longer but on quality, finish, reliability and high technology. This cost many established foreign industry their lives, namely motorcycle manufacturing in Britain and entertainment electronics in America.

Foundations for Economic Success

Japan took advantage of being a late-comer, both in the early preparatory stages of industrialization during the Meiji period and again after 1950. Assisted by world conditions and expansion of demand for precisely the type of products Japan had specialized in, the economy was locked into a virtuous circle of growth. Institutions necessary for industrialization and an infrastructure to promote economic development emerged. There were no religious or caste barriers to the pursuit of material success and no intention of establishing a state-run economy, but rather a protectionist symbiosis of state and private enterprise. A new generation of entrepreneurs emerged in fields such as electronics, cameras, motor cycles and other products which soon flooded the markets of the world.

Crash and Recession

Japan's rapid growth ended in the mid-1990s when the country suffered a major recession from which it has yet to recover. From 1986 to 1991, overconfidence and speculation, in tandem with uncontrolled money supply and credit expansion, inflated real estate and stock market prices. By August 1990, the stock index had plummeted to half its peak. The bursting of the Japanese asset price bubble contributed to what many call the "Lost Decade."

Japan Today

Japan inspired fears of world domination among Western powers after its stellar economic boom, but it is no longer a perceived threat. Still, the economy of Japan is the third largest in the world by nominal GDP[28] and the world's second largest developed economy.[29] Japan is the world's third largest automobile manufacturing country (after China and the USA),[30] has a large consumer electronics industry, and is often ranked among the most innovative countries leading in global patent filings.[31] Facing competition from China and South Korea, manufacturing in Japan today now centers on high-tech and precision goods, such as optical instruments, hybrid vehicles and robotics.

Japan's economic success came with a number of business practices that remain in effect today. A strict corporate hierarchy and life-long employment are the most well-known. Its old-fashioned business culture is a disadvantage for Japanese firms against their challengers in China and South Korea. Japanese bosses, with an average age of sixty, are extremely risk-averse. Years of losses and restructuring make it even harder for them to bet boldly on future technologies. Honoring their culture of lifetime employment, most large Japanese firms have a staff surplus of about one third. They cannot be fired due to the country's unclear labor rules.

Knowing some of the basics of Japanese history helps to understand how its people conduct business and view professional relationships. Even though much has changed in the last fifty years, at their core, most Japanese

---

[28] World Bank. GDP (US) Data by Country (2013). http://data.worldbank.org/indicator/NY.GDP.MKTP.CD.

[29] Organization for Economic Co-operation and Development OECD. Country Statistical Profile: Japan (2013). http://www.oecd-ilibrary.org/economics/country-statistical-profile-japan_20752288-table-jpn.

[30] International Organization of Motor Vehicle Manufacturers OICA. Production Statistics (2013). http://www.oica.net/category/production-statistics/.

[31] World Intellectual Property Organization WIPO. World Intellectual Property Indicators (2013). http://www.wipo.int/ipstats/en/wipi/.

companies and their employees still act like their parents and grandparents. This fits with the contradictory image of Japan as a high-tech country, steeped in ancient rituals and conventions. Keep this in the back of your mind on your journey through this book.

Watch Japanese Movies

More fun than reading about history is watching it. Years after my time in Japan, when I started collecting Japanese movie classics from the 1950s, I recognized many social patterns that I had eluded me before. Like most people, I had only seen the more recent movies from Japan, some ghost and horror stories, historical drama and animation, all of which portray a different country than one finds in reality. It is the older Japanese movies that you should watch to get a better understanding. They often deal with everyday problems of the working class, both in their families and their jobs. Many of the social dynamics have barely changed since, and so have the ways the Japanese cope with them.

Even though most young people point out that their country has completely changed in the last few years, this is a myth. Every single Japanese that I met professed that he or she was different from all the others. After a while, this turned out to be wishful thinking. They *wanted* to be different, radical, daring and forward-looking, but their culture runs so deep that most of them settle in a pre-programmed pattern. I find nothing wrong with tradition, and following in the footsteps of one's parents is perfectly fine. What struck me though was their sheer ambition to be different. At the end of the day, things in Japan have not changed much. Old traditions are still in place and people live by them, mostly without being aware of it.

Japanese entertainment has always attracted international fans among the so-called *Otaku*, avid fans of manga and anime. Sofia Coppola's movie *Lost in Translation*[32] did a lot to promote Japan as a dreamy, enchanted destination to Western audiences. It tells the story of an aging Hollywood actor (Bill Murray) and a recent college graduate (Scarlett Johansson) who develop a rapport after a chance meeting in a Tokyo hotel. But movies made in Japan have enjoyed mainstream success around the world as well. The animation classics by Studio Ghibli, *Princess Mononoke*[33] and *Spirited*

---

[32] Wikipedia. Lost in Translation (2003).
http://en.wikipedia.org/wiki/Lost_in_Translation_%28film%29.
[33] Wikipedia. Princess Mononoke (もののけ姫, Mononoke-hime, 1997).
https://en.wikipedia.org/wiki/Princess_Mononoke.

Away[34] in particular, gained a global fanbase after Disney started their worldwide distribution. Japanese horror movies like *The Ring*[35] and *The Grudge*[36] were equally successful. They were even re-made by Hollywood studios with American actors in Japanese locations. Films by Takeshi Kitano, such as *Battle Royale*[37], *Zatoichi*[38] or his Yakuza movie *Outrage*[39] made a splash far beyond Japan. They are all entertaining, but they portray an unrealistic version of Japan which foreigners fall in love with. When they arrive in the country for a longer stay, it has a rude awakening in store for them.

The older films directed by some of the luminaries of Japanese cinema paint a more realistic picture. When I discovered them, I was surprised how accurately they sketched the modern-day Japan I had encountered. I had no clue that these movies existed when I lived there, mostly because none of my friends had any interest in them. Even those with Masters' degrees in Japan studies had never heard of these movies and were surprised how good they were after I made them watch them. To understand this country and its people better, I recommend you do the same. Here is a short list of movies to help you choose. It also includes one contemporary movie that gives a good outline about life in Tokyo.

Tokyo Story (1953)[40]

This film is a Japanese classic. Directed by Yasujiro Ozu, it tells the story of a couple from the countryside who travel to Tokyo to visit their grown-up children. The film describes their lives and struggles with their identities and daily responsibilities. During the parents' visit, they have little time to entertain them, and only their widowed daughter-in-law (Setsuko Hara) treats them with kindness. This movie shows some of the family dynamics

---

[34] Wikipedia. Spirited Away (千と千尋の神隠し, Sen to Chihiro no Kamikakushi, 2001). https://en.wikipedia.org/wiki/Spirited_Away.

[35] Wikipedia. The Ring (リング, Ringu, 1998). https://en.wikipedia.org/wiki/Ring_%28film%29.

[36] Wikipedia. The Grudge (呪怨じゅおん, Ju-On, 2002). https://en.wikipedia.org/wiki/Ju-on:_The_Grudge.

[37] Wikipedia. Battle Royale (バトル・ロワイアル, Batoru Rowaiaru, 2000). https://en.wikipedia.org/wiki/Battle_Royale.

[38] Wikipedia. Zatoichi (座頭市, Zatoichi, 2003). https://en.wikipedia.org/wiki/Zat%C5%8Dichi_%282003_film%29.

[39] Wikipedia. Outrage (アウトレイジ, Autoreiji, 2010). https://en.wikipedia.org/wiki/Outrage_%282010_film%29.

[40] Wikipedia. Tokyo Story (東京物語, Tokyo Monogatari, 1953). https://en.wikipedia.org/wiki/Tokyo_Story.

taking place in Japan when it awakened as an economic superpower, many of which are still in effect today.

The Life of Oharu (1952)[41]

Set in the Edo period in the seventeenth century, this historical fiction black-and-white film directed by Kenji Mizoguchi tells the life story of a young woman. Being sold to the local lord as a surrogate mother, she becomes a courtesan until her fall from grace when the wife of the ruler becomes jealous. The film examines the issues of different economic classes and rigid hierarchies in Japanese society.

Lightning (1952)[42]

Directed by Mikio Naruse, this movie is about a dysfunctional family where all of the adult siblings have some existential problems. One of them (Hideko Takamine) decides to break the mold and works hard to fashion a better life for her. Even though it is not considered one of the best of Naruse's works, it gives a good impression of what the Japanese families of the post-war period had to deal with. How they solve their problems and their longing for escapism describes well what I believe still goes on in many Japanese households today.

To Live (1952)[43]

A classic directed by Akira Kurosawa, this film tells the story of a middle-aged man who learns about a fatal disease that will end his life within six months. The main protagonist, a government employee in the planning department, feels he has done nothing productive with his life. He embarks on a quest for meaning and finds it in a neglected project to build a public park, which he pushes through relentlessly against all odds. This film lays bare some of the corporate politics in Japan, incompetence through rigid adherence to hierarchies, and how people deal with it to find happiness in their lives.

---

[41] Wikipedia. The Life of Oharu (西鶴一代女, Saikaku Ichidai Onna, 1952). https://en.wikipedia.org/wiki/The_Life_of_Oharu.

[42] Wikipedia. Lightning (稲妻, Inazuma, 1952). https://en.wikipedia.org/wiki/Lightning_%28film%29

[43] Wikipedia. To Live (生きる, Ikiru, 1952). https://en.wikipedia.org/wiki/Ikiru.

Love Strikes (2011)[44]

Directed by Hitoshi One, this drama-comedy portrays the lifestyle and life choices of young people in modern-day Tokyo. The main character is a thirty-year-old virgin and part-time jobber with no clear direction in his life. When he starts work at a magazine his luck with women abruptly changes and he stumbles from one adventure to the next. Even though this is a comedy, it gives an impression of how young people live in modern Japan.

Is it enough to watch a few movies to understand all about Japan and its people? Of course not. I had not seen these movies until after I had been living there, simply because I had no idea they existed. When you have seen at least one of them, the business lessons in this book make more sense.

---

[44] International Movie Database (IMDB). Love Strikes (モテキ,Moteki, 2011). http://www.imdb.com/title/tt1916708/.

ABOUT THE AUTHOR

Atom Alex Helling is an entrepreneur, traveler and observer with an unconventional story. He founded companies in Europe, America and Asia, wrote film scores with the best and pop songs for the worst. While living in Los Angeles, he struck a seven-figure deal with a major record label, won several songwriting competitions and produced a documentary about Japanese manga and anime. Then he moved to Tokyo where he started another venture and lived through a 9.0 earthquake. He is still a songwriter and movie enthusiast. And he is also writing about all of the above.

www.atomalex.com

THANK YOU

Before you go, I would like to say "thank you" for purchasing my book. It has been a lot of fun to write, and I hope it was fun to read as well.

Now I would like ask for a small favor. If you enjoyed this book, would you please take a minute or two and leave a review on Amazon. This feedback will help me continue to write the kind of books that entertain and help you get results. And if you loved it, then please let me know. I look forward to hearing from you.

STAY IN TOUCH

To stay in the loop about upcoming books and specials, please sign up for my mailing list on **www.atomalex.com/newsletter**. I am always offering free (or deeply discounted) books to my list. And as a subscriber, you will be the first to know about these special deals.

I look forward to hearing from you. If you have any questions or comments, please reach out to me in any of the following ways:

Website: www.atomalex.com
Email: contact@atomalex.com
Twitter: @atomalexhelling
Facebook: www.facebook.com/pages/Atom-Alex-Helling/340442666122299

MORE BOOKS BY ATOM ALEX HELLING

Business Lessons from Hollywood: What I Learned in the Capital of Entertainment

This is a book about doing business Hollywood-style, anywhere in the world, in any industry. Atom Alex Helling, an entrepreneur and music producer, recounts his adventures in the film and music industry in Los Angeles. He distills from them over seventy unexpected business lessons that are easy to apply in any line of work.

"I moved to Los Angeles to break into the music business. Seven years later I had succeeded. In the process I discovered how Hollywood operates. These are the strategies I still apply today."

www.atomalex.com/business-lessons-hollywood

www.ingramcontent.com/pod-product-compliance
Lightning Source LLC
Chambersburg PA
CBHW071801200526
45167CB00017B/749